THE KEY TO FRENCH GRAMMAR

Ian Lan

Text © Ian Lane 1994

Original line illustrations © Mary Glasgow Publications 1994

The right of Ian Lane to be identified as author of this work has been asserted by him in accordance with the Copyright, Designs and Patents Act 1988.

All rights reserved. No part of this publication may be reproduced or transmitted in any form or by any means, electronic or mechanical, including photocopy, recording or any information storage and retrieval system, without permission in writing from the publisher or under licence from the Copyright Licensing Agency Limited. Further details of such licences (for reprographic reproduction) may be obtained from the Copyright Licensing Agency Limited, of Saffron House, 6-10 Kirby Street, London EC1N 8TS.

First published in 1994 by:
Mary Glasgow Publications, an imprint of Stanley Thornes (Publishers) Ltd
Reprinted in 2002 by:
Nelson Thornes Ltd
Delta Place
27 Bath Road
CHELTENHAM
GL53 7TH
United Kingdom

09 10 11 12 / 25 24 23 22 21 20 19

A catalogue record for this book is available from the British Library.

ISBN 978 1 85234 553 2

Illustrations by Shaun Williams
Typeset by Tech-Set, Gateshead, Tyne and Wear
Printed by Multivista Global Ltd

Contents

Introduction

This reference book is mainly written for those of you studying French in the 11 to 16 age range, and also for anyone studying French who wants to be led through the essential elements of French grammar. *The Key to French Grammar* will help you to become more confident users of the language, enabling you to consolidate and revise language points of which you may be unsure.

You will be able to use this reference independently of a teacher:

- Explanations of each grammatical point are given in English.
- Answers are provided so that you may monitor your own progress.
- Use the Contents list to help you to locate specific grammar points.
- Short exercises enable you to practise each point.
- **Tu comprends?** sections help you to test whether or not you have understood.

While you may be required to work your way through the exercises by a teacher, or you might choose yourself to forge ahead and learn more about the language, *The Key to French Grammar* is essentially a reference, aimed at helping you in your hour of need.

Bonne chance et amusez-vous bien!

1 Using *le* and *la*

1 ***Le*** and ***la*** both mean 'the'. ***Le*** words are masculine and ***la*** words are feminine. From the words below, make a list on the left-hand side of your page of all the masculine words and on the right-hand side of all the feminine words.

le parking	la poste
la boulangerie	le parc
la gare	le camping
le supermarché	la piscine
le restaurant	la banque

2 When you look up a word in a dictionary you will notice that it will have either ***nm*** (for a noun that is masculine) after it, or ***nf*** (for a noun that is feminine). ***nm*** will therefore mean that it is a ***le*** (masculine) word and ***nf*** will mean that it is a ***la*** (feminine) word.

3 When a noun begins with a vowel sound (a, e, i, o, u), you put ***l'*** before the word, instead of ***le*** or ***la***.

Example

l'épicerie	*the grocer's*
l'église	*the church*

Most words beginning with ***h*** also follow this pattern because the ***h*** is silent, or not pronounced, and so the words still begin with a vowel sound.

Example

l'hôpital	*the hospital*

4 ***Tu comprends?***

Put either ***le*** or ***la*** in front of the following place names and write down their English meanings. Be careful - there is also one which takes ***l'***. See if you can spot it. Look at the examples first.

Example

parking (***nm***)	= le parking	= *the car park*
poste (***nf***)	= la poste	= *the post office*

Now see if you can do the rest:

a café (**nm**) =
b camping (**nm**) =
c piscine (**nf**) =
d collège (**nm**) =
e port (**nm**) =
f boucherie (**nf**) =
g cinéma (**nm**) =
h église (**nf**) =
i tabac (**nm**) =
j hôtel (**nm**) =

1 SOMMAIRE Using *le* and *la*

1 ***Le***, ***la*** and ***l'*** mean 'the'.

2 All nouns (names of things) in French are either masculine or feminine.

3 Words with ***le*** in front of them are masculine.

4 Words with ***la*** in front of them are feminine.

5 Words with ***l'*** in front of them can be either masculine or feminine

2 Using *un* and *une*

1 There are two words for 'a' or 'an' in French: ***un*** or ***une***. Words that have ***un*** in front of them are masculine (the ***le*** words) and words which have ***une*** in front of them are feminine (the ***la*** words).

Make a list on the left-hand side of your page of all the masculine words and on the right-hand side of all the feminine words contained in these two lists:

un T-shirt	une chaussure
une chemise	un anorak
une chaussette	un jean
un blouson	une cravate
un soutien-gorge	une blouse

2 Remember that when you look up a word in a dictionary you will notice that it will have **nm** (for a noun that is masculine) or **nf** (for a noun that is feminine) after it. In this case, **nm** will mean that it is a word which takes ***un*** and **nf** will mean that it is a word which takes ***une***.

3 Tu comprends?

Put either ***un*** or ***une*** in front of the following articles of clothing and write down their English meanings. The first two have been done for you:

Example

blouson (**nm**)	= un blouson	= *a jacket*
cravate (**nf**)	= une cravate	= *a tie*

Now see if you can do the rest:

a soutien-gorge (**nm**) =
b pantalon (**nm**) =
c jupe (**nf**) =
d chapeau (**nm**) =
e manteau (**nm**) =
f robe (**nf**) =
g anorak (**nm**) =
h ceinture (**nf**) =
i short (**nm**) =
j survêtement (**nm**) =

2 SOMMAIRE Using *un* and *une*

1 All nouns (names of things) in French are either masculine or feminine.

2 Words with ***un*** in front of them are masculine.

3 Words with ***une*** in front of them are feminine.

4 Both ***un*** and ***une*** mean 'a' or 'an'. So:

un cinéma	*a cinema*	le cinéma	*the cinema*
une église	*a church*	l'église	*the church*

Extra note

Some words that look the same but have a different gender (***un*** instead of ***une***, or vice versa) actually have quite a different meaning:

un livre	*a book*
une livre	*a pound*

3 Using *les* and *des*

1 Using ***les*** and ***des*** can help you talk about more than one of those nouns mentioned in Points 1 and 2 by:

a Adding an **s** and using the word ***les*** (the) in front of it.
b By adding an **s** and using the word ***des*** (some) in front of it.

Example

les stylos	*the pens*
des stylos	*some pens*
les ordinateurs	*the computers*
des ordinateurs	*some computers*

2 Write out the following list, filling in the blanks with either 'some', 'the', ***des*** or ***les*** as you go. The first two have been done for you. Don't forget to check your answers.

a	*some rulers*	des règles
b	*the rulers*	les règles
c	..... *rubbers*	les gommes
d	..... *pencils*	des crayons
e	*the textbooks*	..... livres
f	*some cassettes*	..... cassettes
g	..... *disks*	les disquettes
h	..... *felt-tip pens*	des feutres
i	..... *exercise books*	les cahiers
j	*the tape recorders*	..... magnétophones

3 Tu comprends?
Choose the correct word from the box below to complete the following sentences. Some of the words have to be used more than once. When you have finished, check your answers.

a Où sont ..... toilettes (*the toilets*)?
b Est-ce qu'il y a ..... café près d'ici (*a café*)?
c Je vais à ..... hôpital (*the hospital*).

d Où est ..... cinéma (*the cinéma*)?
e Il y a ..... taxis (*some taxis*) en face de la gare.
f Est-ce qu'il y a ..... boulangerie (*a baker's*) en ville?
g ..... poste (*the post-office*) est à deux minutes d'ici.
h J'aime beaucoup ..... marché (*the market*) en ville.
i Où est ..... boucherie (*the butcher's*)?
j S'il vous plaît, il y a ..... téléphone (*a phone*) ici?

Extra note
In most cases, you have to add an **s** to French nouns to make them plural (more than one). There are some nouns that do not follow this rule. The two following patterns are among some of the exceptions. All exceptions have to be learned separately:

a add **x** to words that end in ***u***:

un château	→	les/des châteaux
un jeu	→	les/des jeux
un chou	→	les/des choux

b change words that end in ***al*** to ***aux***:

un hôpital	→	les/des hôpitaux
un animal	→	les/des animaux

There are fortunately few exceptions to these patterns. Amongst these exceptions are the following plural words:

les fous	*the mad people*
les cous	*the necks*
les bals	*the dances/balls*
les carnavals	*the carnivals*

Note
Some words are more commonly used in their plural form. When you look these words up in a dictionary, you will notice the letters ***nmpl*** or ***nfpl*** after the word, to remind you not only of the word's gender, but that it is used in its plural form. For example, les vacances ***nfpl*** (holidays).

3 SOMMAIRE Using *les* and *des*

1 When you see the words **des** or **les** in front of a noun in French, it means that there is more than one of that item.

2 ***Des*** means 'some' and ***les*** means 'the'.

3 In most cases, you also add an **s** to a noun to make it plural (more than one).

Example

un stylo	*a pen*
le stylo	*the pen*
les stylos	*the pens*
des stylos	*some pens*

... but don't forget to remember the exceptions!

4 Note that in English we often do not use 'some' or 'the'. In French, you can not do without ***les*** or ***des***:

Example

Have you got pens?	Vous avez des stylos?
Have you got pencils?	Vous avez des crayons?
I like flowers.	J'aime les fleurs.
I don't like maths.	Je n'aime pas les maths.

4 Adjectives

1 Adjectives are words that describe things. In French, adjectives change their spelling according to whether they are describing something/someone masculine or feminine. Look below:

Il est **grand**	mais	elle est **grande**.
Il est **petit**	mais	elle est **petite**.
Il est **intelligent**	mais	elle est **intelligente**.
Il est **fort**	mais	elle est **forte**.
Il est **mince**	et	elle est **mince**.
Il est **marié**	mais	elle est **mariée**.

The words in bold type are adjectives, i.e. they describe what ***il*** and ***elle*** (he and she) are like. Notice that when adjectives describe someone or something which is feminine, you add an **e**.

There are unfortunately a few exceptions:

a Don't add an **e** if there already is one at the end of the adjective, such as ***mince***.

b You still add an **e** if the word ends in **é**, such as ***marié***.

c Some adjectives follow an irregular pattern, so it's not always just a question of adding an **e** for the feminine adjective ending:

adjective describing masculine object/person		*adjective describing feminine object/person*
blanc	→	blanche (*white*)
gros	→	grosse (*fat*)
bon	→	bonne (*good*)
mignon	→	mignonne (*cute*)
long	→	longue (*long*)
beau	→	belle (*good-looking/beautiful*)
délicieux	→	délicieuse (*delicious*)
rêveur	→	rêveuse (*dreamy, a dreamer*)
vieux	→	vieille (*old*)

2 Write out the following descriptions, selecting the correct spellings:

a J'ai un éléphant. Il s'appelle Pierre. Il est très grand/grande et très gros/grosse. De couleur, il est gris/grise.

b Voici ma voiture noir/noire et blanc/blanche. Elle est superbe. Elle est très grand/grande. Elle est aussi très confortable.
c J'ai une souris. Elle s'appelle Sauvage. Elle est petit/petite, blanc/blanche et méchant/méchante. Elle attaque les éléphants!

3 When adjectives describe someone or something which is plural (more than one), you add an **s**.

Example
Il est grand mais ils sont grand**s**.
Elle est grand**e** mais elles sont grand**es**.

However, note that you don't add anything if the word used to describe (adjective) an object/person ends in an **x** or an **s** already.

Example

il est merveilleux	ils sont merveilleux (*marvellous*)
il est gris	ils sont gris (*grey*)

4 Tu comprends?
Help hippy Dylan to describe himself and his pet rabbit accurately, by choosing one of the words in bold type where appropriate:

Je m'appelle Dylan. Je suis **grand/grande**. Je suis mince. J'ai les cheveux **long/longs** et **blond/blonds**. J'ai les yeux **bleu/bleus**. J'ai un visage **long/longue**.

Voici mon lapin. Il s'appelle Jake. Il est **petit/petite**. Il est **blanc/blanche**. Il est **végétarien/végétarienne**. Il est **mignon/mignonne**. Il est un peu **gros/grosse**. Il adore les carottes.

... Now check your answers.

4 SOMMAIRE Adjectives

1 Adjectives must agree with the things or people they describe.

Add nothing when masculine:	Le bateau est grand.
Add **e** when feminine:	La voiture est grand**e**.
Add **s** when plural:	Les bateaux sont grand**s**.
Add **es** when feminine and plural:	Les voitures sont grand**es**.

2 Watch out for exceptions which need to be learned separately.

5 Understanding what a verb is

1 The verb is the word in the sentence which tells you what is happening or what action is taking place. It's sometimes referred to as the 'doing word'. See if you can work out which word in each of the sentences is the verb.

Il joue au football.

Elle regarde la télévision.

Ils travaillent.

Elles dansent.

Yes, you guessed it! The verbs were ***joue*** (plays), ***regarde*** (watches), ***travaillent*** (work) and ***dansent*** (dance).

2 Give these cartoons the right captions from the sentences in the box:

Il écoute la radio.	**Elle mange du fromage.**
Ils jouent au tennis.	**Ils dansent un slow.**
Elle chante à l'opéra.	

3 Different person words ('subject pronouns') can be used with verbs to indicate who does the action. Look at the speech bubbles opposite.

4 From the cartoons above, see if you can match up the following French subject pronouns with the English. You will notice that there are two words for 'you' and two words for 'they'. The first one has been done for you.

je	**he**
tu	**she**
ils	**they**
elle	**we**
vous	**you**
nous	**they**
il	**I**
elles	**you**

Example
je = *I*

5 Tu comprends?

Match the captions in the box below with the pictures of tennis players as accurately as you can.

Elles jouent au tennis. Je joue au tennis. Il joue au tennis.
Nous jouons au tennis. Vous jouez au tennis?
Elle joue au tennis. Ils jouent au tennis. Tu joues au tennis?

... Now check your answers!

5 SOMMAIRE Understanding what a verb is

1 The verb is the word in a sentence which tells you what is happening or what's going on, sometimes called the 'doing word'.

2 To show who or what is doing the action, verbs are used with different subject pronouns ('person words'):

je	*I*
tu	*you*
il	*he*
elle	*she*
on	*'one'* (see point 5 below)
nous	*we*
vous	*you*
ils	*they*
elles	*they*

3 There are two words for 'you': ***tu*** and ***vous***.

a ***Tu*** is the more familiar way of addressing somebody. Use ***tu*** when speaking to one other person whom you would normally call by their first name or a person of the same family as yourself.

b ***Vous*** is the more formal way of addressing somebody. You use ***vous*** when addressing a group of people or an adult with whom you are not on first name terms, such as a teacher or a somebody you have not met before.

4 There are two words for 'they': ***ils*** and ***elles***.

a You use ***ils*** when talking about a group of males, or a group or combination of male and female people or things.

b You use ***elles*** when talking about a group of female people or things.

5 ***On*** takes the same spelling of the verb as ***il*** or ***elle***. It is sometimes referred to as meaning 'one', as in 'one does this and one does that'. However, it is more commonly used in French than in English, and it is used in a variety of ways:

a In questions:

On va au cinéma?	*Shall we go to the pictures?*
On joue au football?	*Shall we play football?*

b It is also used to talk about what 'we' do:

On regarde la télé.	*We watch/are watching TV.*

Look out for its use!

c ***Ils*** also means 'they' when referring to a male/female mix:

Où sont Monique et Pierre? Ils regardent la télé.
Where are Monique and Pierre? They are watching TV.

6 Using regular -er verbs in the Present Tense

1 Most verbs that you will come across in French are regular **-er** verbs. They are called this because:

a The infinitives end in **-er**: *jou**er**, regard**er**, écout**er***, etc.

b They follow a regular pattern.

When the verb still has the **-er** attached to it, it is known as the 'infinitive'.

jou**er**	***to** play*
regard**er**	***to** watch*
écout**er**	***to** listen to*

2 Before you use any of these verbs in the Present Tense you must break down the verb. In other words, you take off the **-er** and add the ending you need:

Example

je joue	*I play/am playing/do play*
tu joues	*you play/are playing/do play*
il/elle/on joue	*he/she/one plays/is playing/does play*
nous jouons	*we play/are playing/do play*
vous jouez	*you play/are playing/do play*
ils/elles jouent	*they play/are playing/do play*

All other regular **-er** verbs follow this pattern. The endings are important and must be learned thoroughly. Here are some regular **-er** verbs you've probably already met, but there are many more.

aimer	*to like/to love*
arriver	*to arrive*
chanter	*to sing*
danser	*to dance*
écouter	*to listen to*
entrer	*to enter*
habiter	*to live in*

jouer	*to play*
parler	*to speak*
pêcher	*to fish*
regarder	*to watch*
rester	*to stay*
travailler	*to work*

3 See how much you already understand by completing the following sentences with the right endings or the right subject pronouns (person words). Don't forget to check your answers.

a ..... écoutons de la musique.
b J'aim..... la musique.
c ..... danses?
d Pierre travaill..... dans le jardin.
e Elle regard..... la télé.
f Ils rest..... à la maison.
g ..... parlez français?
h Elles jou..... au tennis.
i Ma mère et moi écout..... la radio.
j Monique travaill..... au collège.

4 Tu comprends?

Complete the story, for each gap selecting the appropriate infinitive verb from the box below and putting it into the correct verb form.

aimer	**arriver**	**entrer**	**chanter**
danser	**écouter**	**pêcher**	**regarder**

J' ..... les samedis. Mes amis (ils) ..... à la maison à dix heures. Nous ..... la télévision pendant trois heures. À une heure je prends un hamburger-frites. L'après-midi, je vais à la pêche avec mes copains. Nous ..... les truites. Mon père reste à la maison. Il ..... la radio et il ..... avec ses disques préférés. Ma mère ..... . Elle adore danser. Le soir, je ..... un bon film à la télé. J' ..... dans ma chambre vers dix heures, j' ..... la radio et je m'endors____zzzz!

6 SOMMAIRE Using regular -er verbs in the Present Tense

1 Regular ***-er*** verbs are called this because:

a The infinitives end in ***-er***: ***jouer***, ***regarder***, ***écouter***, etc.
b The endings of these verbs follow a regular pattern. Remove the ***-er*** from the infinitive and add the right endings:

je joue	*I play/am playing/do play*
tu joues	*you play/are playing/do play*
il/elle/on joue	*he/she/one plays/is playing/does play*
nous jouons	*we play/are playing/do play*
vous jouez	*you play/are playing/do play*
ils/elles jouent	*they play/are playing/do play*

Note
You must thoroughly learn these endings if you are to use the language confidently.

2 Note that there is only one way of expressing the Present Tense in French: ***je joue*** means either 'I play', 'I am playing' or 'I do play'.

3 Note that when you look up a verb in a dictionary it will be in the infinitive: ***regarder***, ***acheter***, ***écouter***, etc. This applies to all types of verbs.

7 Using regular *-ir* and *-re* verbs in the Present Tense

1 As well as regular **-er** verbs (see Point 6), there are also regular **-ir** verbs and regular **-re** verbs. There are many fewer of these.

a The infinitives of regular **-ir** verbs end in **-ir**: ***finir***, ***choisir***, ***rougir***, etc.
b The infinitives of regular **-re** verbs end in **-re**: **vendre**, **attendre**, **répondre**, etc.

2 Regular **-ir** and **-re** verbs follow regular patterns when they are broken down.

a To use a regular **-ir** verb, such as **finir**, take off the **-ir** and add the right ending:

je fin***is***	*I finish/am finishing/do finish*
tu fin***is***	*you finish/are finishing/do finish*
il/elle/on fin***it***	*he/she/one finishes/is finishing/does finish*
nous fin***issons***	*we finish/are finishing/do finish*
vous fin***issez***	*you finish/are finishing/do finish*
ils/elles fin***issent***	*they finish/are finishing/do finish*

b A regular **-re** verb, such as **vendre**, takes the following pattern: take off the **-re** and add the right ending:

je vend***s***	*I sell/am selling/do sell*
tu vend***s***	*you sell/are selling/do sell*
il/elle/on vend	*he/she/one sells/is selling/does sell*
nous vend***ons***	*we sell/are selling/do sell*
vous vend***ez***	*you sell/are selling/do sell*
ils/elles vend***ent***	*they sell/are selling/do sell*

c Here are some fairly common regular **-ir** and regular **-re** verbs:

-ir

choisir	*to choose*
finir	*to finish*
grandir	*to grow*
rougir	*to blush*
vomir	*to be sick*
obéir	*to obey*

-re

attendre	*to wait for*
perdre	*to lose*
répondre	*to answer*
vendre	*to sell*

3 Using the notes above, match up the words in the left-hand box with those in the right-hand box:

je il nous
vous ils tu
elle nous
vous elles

choisis un disque rougissons
obéissent vomit finissez
répondent en français
attendons un bus vendez la maison
répond à ma lettre perds tes devoirs

4 Tu comprends?

Complete this story by changing the verb from the infinitive into the correct verb form. Look out for all the regular ***-er***, ***-ir*** and ***-re*** verbs.

Une histoire d'amour

C'est vendredi le vingt-quatre décembre. Je m'appelle Jean Saitro. Je suis cool. J'(arriver) à la disco avec mes copains. Il y a une jeune fille qui danse. Elle s'appelle Céline Bisou. Elle est magnifique. Céline (danser) et moi, je (parler) avec mes copains. Elle (adorer) danser. Plus tard, je (choisir) un disque pour Céline. Elle est très contente. Nous (danser) le slow ensemble. Je (rougir). La disco (finir) vers onze heures. Nous (rentrer) à mobylette ensemble. Mes copains (attendre) le bus. Je suis amoureux.

Don't forget to check your answers!

7 SOMMAIRE Using regular *-ir* and *-re* verbs in the Present Tense

1 Regular ***-ir*** verb infinitives end in ***-ir***: ***finir***, ***choisir***, etc. Like regular **-er** verbs, they follow a regular pattern. Take off the ***-ir*** and add the following endings: ***is***, ***is***, ***it***, ***issons***, ***issez***, ***issent***.

2 Regular ***-re*** verb infinitives end in ***-re***: **vendre**, **attendre**, etc. Like regular **-er** and ***-ir*** verbs, they follow a regular pattern, but with the following endings: **s**, **s**, (nothing), **ons**, **ez**, **ent**.

3 Again, these endings have to be learned thoroughly.

8 Using irregular verbs in the Present Tense

1 Not all verbs follow a regular pattern like those in Points 6 and 7. Those that don't follow a regular pattern are known as 'irregular verbs', and these have to be learned separately.

2 These are some of the most common ones:

être	*to be*	*avoir*	*to have*
je suis	*I am*	j'ai	*I have/am having, etc*
tu es	*you are*	tu as	*you have*
il/elle/on est	*he/she/one is*	il/elle/on a	*he/she/one has*
nous sommes	*we are*	nous avons	*we have*
vous êtes	*you are*	vous avez	*you have*
ils/elles sont	*they are*	ils/elles ont	*they have*
aller	*to go*	*prendre*	*to take*
je vais	*I go/am going, etc*	je prends	*I take/am taking, etc*
tu vas	*you go*	tu prends	*you take*
il/elle/on va	*he/she/one goes*	il/elle/on prend	*he/she/one takes*
nous allons	*we go*	nous prenons	*we take*
vous allez	*you go*	vous prenez	*you take*
ils/elles vont	*they go*	ils/elles prennent	*they take*

faire	*to do, to make*
je fais	*I do/make, I am doing/making, etc*
tu fais	*you do/make*
il/elle/on fait	*he/she/one does/makes*
nous faisons	*we do/make*
vous faites	*you do/make*
ils/elles font	*they do/make*

3 Complete the following sentences using the correct spelling of **être**.

a Il ..... au cinéma.
b Nous ..... à la piscine.
c Ils ..... au café.
d Elle ..... au restaurant.
e Elles ..... aux toilettes.
f Je ..... à la gare.
g Vous ..... au pub.
h Tu ..... au match de foot?
i Je ..... à Paris.
j Ils ..... en France.

4 On five occasions, an incorrect verb form of ***avoir*** has been used in the following sentences. What should have been written? To help you, the verb form of ***avoir*** has been emboldened in each sentence.

a Il **ai** un ordinateur.
b Nous **avez** des biscuits.
c Ils **ont** des bonbons.
d Elle **avons** un chien.
e Elles **ont** des chips.
f J'**ai** une perruche.
g Vous **avez** des bananes.
h Tu **avez** une bicyclette?
i J'**ai** des devoirs.
j Ils **avez** des oignons.

5 Some of the verbs and subject pronouns are missing. Complete the following sentences with the correct spelling of ***aller***, or the correct subject pronoun.

a Il ..... au cinéma.
b ..... allons à la piscine.
c Ils ..... au café.
d Elle ..... au restaurant.
e Elles ..... aux toilettes.
f ..... vais à la gare.
g ..... allez au musée.
h ..... vas au match de foot?
i Je ..... à Paris.
j Ils ..... en France.

6 Fill in the missing letters to complete the different spellings of ***prendre***:

a Je _ r_nd_ mon petit déjeuner.
b Nous p_en_n_ le train.
c Elle _r_n_ une douche.
d Vous _r_ne_ un café?
e Tu p_e_ds le bus?
f Ils p_en_e_t le taxi.

7 List the verb ***faire*** in full without looking at your notes above if you can manage it.

8 Tu comprends?

Complete this story about Chris' routine while staying with a family in France. Change the infinitives. Look out for the irregular as well as regular verbs! Use the notes in this Point, as well as preceeding Points, to help you.

Je me réveille à sept heures. Je (prendre) une douche et je (prendre) mon petit déjeuner. J'adore les croissants! Je (aller) au collège avec mon correspondant. Nous (attendre) le bus. Les cours (commencer) à 8 heures. Je (être) très fatigué. Nous (prendre) le déjeuner à midi. À cinq heures, les cours (finir) et nous (quitter) le collège. À la maison, nous (faire) nos devoirs. Nous (faire) la vaisselle après le dîner. Je (aller) au lit vers dix heures.

8 SOMMAIRE Using irregular verbs in the Present Tense

Not all verbs follow a regular pattern. These are known as irregular verbs and they have to be learned separately.

9 Using reflexive verbs in the Present Tense

1 Reflexive verbs can be recognised in the infinitive form (see Point 6) because they have **se** in front of them:

Example

se réveiller	*to wake (oneself) up*
se lever	*to get (oneself) up*
se raser	*to shave (oneself)*
se laver	*to wash (oneself)*
s'habiller	*to dress (oneself)*
se coucher	*to go to bed*
se promener	*to go for a walk*

It's worth remembering that in general those things to do with getting up in the morning and last thing at night are 'reflexive'.

2 Note, you can also turn verbs which are not usually reflexive into reflexives, if the action is done to yourself, his/herself, etc.:

Example

je me regarde	*I look at myself*
je me dis	*I say to myself*

But be careful! Treating all verbs like this can result in nonsense:

je me mange	*I eat myself*

3 Notice that each of the person words needs a 'reflexive pronoun'. In the following example, the reflexive pronouns are highlighted in bold type.

je **me** lave	*I wash (myself)*
tu **te** laves	*you wash (yourself)*
il/elle/on **se** lave	*he/she/one washes (himself, herself, oneself)*
nous **nous** lavons	*we wash (ourselves)*
vous **vous** lavez	*you wash (yourself, yourselves)*
ils/elles **se** lavent	*they wash (themselves)*

Other reflexive verbs work in the same way.

4 Write out the following sentences in the right order. Don't forget to check your answers. The first one has been done for you.

a je / lave / me = je me lave
b ils / lavent / se
c réveilles / te / tu / huit / à / heures
d elle / lève / se / à / heures / sept
e il / s' / à / sept / habille / heures
f elle / promène / se / neuf / à / heures
g couche / me / je / à / heures / neuf / demie / et
h nous / à / heures / six / réveillons / nous
i rase / se / il / à / heures / sept / demie / et
j couchez / vous / dix / heures? / à / vous

5 Tu comprends?

Complete the following sentences using the symbols as a guide to what you should write:

a Je ..... à sept heures.

b Ils ..... à six heures.

c  Vous ..... à huit heures.

d  Nous.....à sept heures dix.

e  Tu ..... à sept heures et quart.

f Elle ..... à dix heures.

g Il ..... à sept heures.

h  On ..... à six heures et demie.

i  Nous ..... à trois heures.

j  Ils ..... à minuit.

9 SOMMAIRE Using reflexive verbs in the Present Tense

1 Reflexive infinitives can be recognised from the **se** in front of them:

se réveiller — *to wake up*
se coucher — *to go to bed*

2 Reflexive verbs require a reflexive pronoun.

je **me** couche	*I go to bed*
tu **te** couches	*you go to bed*
il/elle/on **se** couche	*he/she/one goes to bed*
nous **nous** couchons	*we go to bed*
vous **vous** couchez	*you go to bed*
ils/elles **se** couchent	*they go to bed*

3 Other verbs can also be made reflexive.

je me regarde — *I look at myself*
je m'écoute — *I listen to myself*

but be careful to avoid nonsense such as **Je me mange**!

4 Also, note how you would say the following:

Je me lave **les** cheveux. — *I wash my hair.*
Je me brosse **les** dents. — *I brush my teeth.*
Je me casse **la** jambe. — *I break my leg.*

10 Using *ne... pas*

1 If you want to make a negative statement in French (for example, 'I don't like coffee', or 'She is not singing'), you must put ***ne*** before the verb and ***pas*** after the verb.

Example

je danse	*I dance* or *I am dancing*
je **ne** danse **pas**	*I **don't** dance* or *I am **not** dancing*

When the verb begins with a vowel, the ***ne*** becomes ***n'***.

Example

Je **n'**aime pas les frites.	*I don't like chips.*
Je **n'**écoute pas la radio.	*I don't listen to the radio/I'm not listening to the radio.*

2 Make the following statements negative by using ***ne*** and ***pas***:

a Je joue au football.
b Elle regarde la télé.
c Nous écoutons la radio.
d Il danse à la disco.
e Reste à la maison!
f Je parle français.
g Prenez le bus!
h J'aime les sciences.
i Tu comprends?
j Vous aimez les frites?

Now check your answers.

3 Tu comprends?
Your friend is going to France and she doesn't speak much French. You've been asked to write a brief resumé about what she likes and dislikes and what she does and doesn't do. You have to work from her notes. The first few have been done for you.

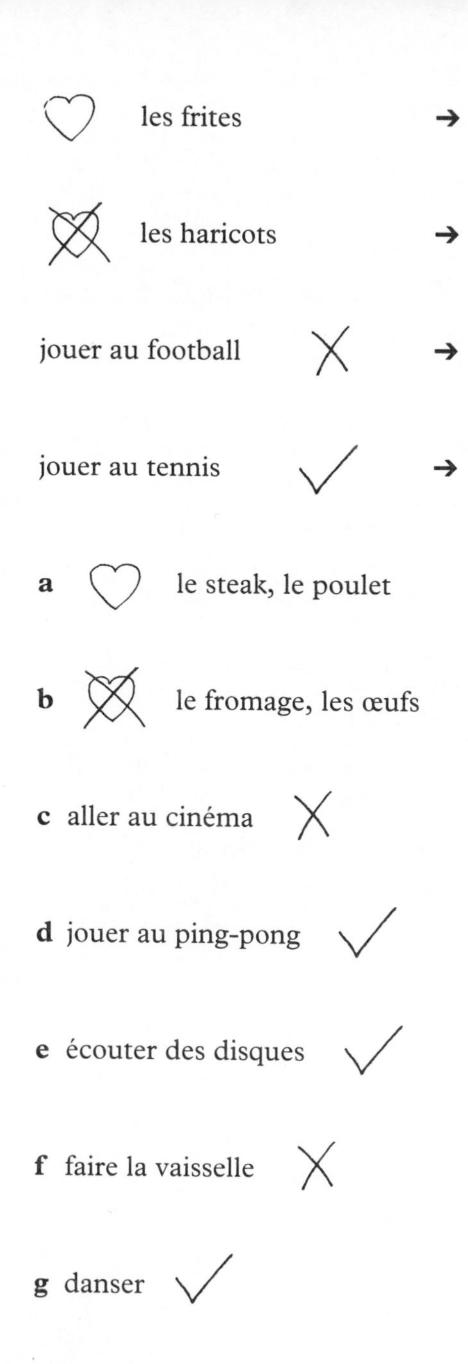

les frites → Elle aime les frites.

les haricots → Elle n'aime pas les haricots.

jouer au football → Elle ne joue pas au football.

jouer au tennis → Elle joue au tennis.

a le steak, le poulet

b le fromage, les œufs

c aller au cinéma

d jouer au ping-pong

e écouter des disques

f faire la vaisselle

g danser

h regarder la télé

10 SOMMAIRE using *ne... pas*

1 If you want to talk about 'not doing' something in French, or in other words to make a negative statement, you need two words: ***ne*** and ***pas***.

2 ***Ne*** is placed before the verb and ***pas*** comes after the verb:

je comprends	*I understand*
je **ne** comprends **pas**	***I don't*** *understand*

3 Don't forget that when a verb begins with a vowel, the **ne** becomes ***n'***:

J'aime le français.	*I like French.*
Je **n'**aime **pas** le français.	***I don't*** *like French.*

4 Note that ***pas*** can be used on its own with nouns to form commonly used expressions:

Pas de problème!	*No problem!*
Pas de chance!	*Unlucky! (No luck!)*

5 Note also that, in negative statements, **de** has to be used after the ***pas*** in place of ***du***, ***de la***, ***des***, ***un*** or ***une***:

Tu as **une** voiture?	Non, je n'ai pas **de** voiture!
Vous avez **du** sucre?	Non, nous n'avons pas **de** sucre!

11 Asking questions

1 There are three ways of asking questions in French:

a By making your voice go up at the end of an ordinary sentence. This is used a lot in conversation.

Example

Tu habites à Paris? — *Do you live in Paris?*
Vous êtes anglais? — *Are you English?*
Il est huit heures? — *Is it eight o'clock?*

b By using ***est-ce que*** at the start of a statement:

Example

Est-ce que tu habites à Paris? — *Do you live in Paris?*
Est-ce que vous êtes anglais? — *Are you English?*
Est-ce qu'il est huit heures? — *Is it eight o'clock?*

c By turning the verb round (though much less common than the other two ways of asking questions, especially in speech):

Example

Habites-tu à Paris? — *Do you live in Paris?*
Êtes-vous anglais? — *Are you English?*
Est-il huit heures? — *Is it eight o'clock?*

Note that when the verb ends in a vowel with ***il*** or ***elle***, you need to add an extra ***t***. This is just to ease pronunciation:

Example

Habite-**t**-il à Paris? — *Does he live in Paris?*
Joue-**t**-elle au football? — *Does she play football?*

In the Past Perfect Tense (see Points 23-26), you just invert or turn round the auxiliary verb (***avoir*** or ***être***):

Example

Avez-vous habité à Paris? — *Have you lived in Paris?*
Êtes-vous arrivé en Angleterre? — *Have you reached England?*

Again, a ***t*** is added for pronunciation with ***il*** or ***elle*** when ***avoir*** is used as the auxiliary:

Example

A-**t**-il habité à Paris?	*Has he lived in Paris?*
A-**t**-elle joué au football?	*Has she played football?*

2 Use the following questions to try to work out what the statements are. The first one has been done for you. Don't forget to check your answers in the back of the book:

a Habite-t-il en France? = Il habite en France.
b Joue-t-elle au football?
c Est-ce qu'il parle français?
d Tu aimes la glace au chocolat?
e Habites-tu en Angleterre?
f Est-ce qu'elle aime le collège?
g Fais-tu tes devoirs?
h Est-ce que vous aimez le français?

Try these two in the Past Perfect Tense:

i As-tu été en France?
j As-tu choisi?

3 You can ask even more if you understand certain key question words:

où	*where*
que	*what* (shortened to **qu'** with **est-ce que**)
qui	*who*
quand	*when*
comment	*how*
combien	*how much, how many*
pourquoi	*why*
à quelle heure	*at what time*
avec qui	*with whom*
quel (*m*)	*which/what.* Notice this changes like an adjective:
quelle (*f*)	
quels (*mpl*)	
quelles (*fpl*)	

4 Tu comprends?

Complete each of the reporter's questions with the correct question words:

La journaliste	*La Reine Elizabeth*
a ..... vous appelez-vous?	Je m'appelle la Reine Elizabeth.
b ..... habitez-vous exactement?	J'habite à Buckingham Palace.
c ..... d'enfants avez-vous?	J'en ai quatre.
d ..... est le plus âgé?	C'est Charles.
e ..... allez-vous en vacances?	Au mois de février.
f ..... ?	Avec mon mari.
g ..... est la date de votre voyage?	C'est le 10 février.
h ..... allez-vous?	Nous allons en Australie.
i ..... ?	Parce qu'il fait chaud là bas.
Merci de votre gentillesse, au revoir.	Au revoir jeune homme.

11 SOMMAIRE Asking questions

1 There are three ways of asking questions in French:

- **a** By raising your voice at the end of the sentence in a questioning way.
- **b** By adding **est-ce que** to the beginning of the sentence.
- **c** By turning the verb round.

2 Remember that you turn the auxiliary round in the past tense:

Avez-vous fini votre travail?	*Have you finished your work?*
As-tu décidé?	*Have you decided?*

3 You can ask many more interesting things by adding the right question words.

12 Words for 'my', 'your', 'his' and 'her'

1 There are three words for 'my' in French: ***mon***, ***ma*** and ***mes***.

Example

mon père	*my father*
ma mère	*my mother*
mes parents	*my parents*

So, ***mon*** is used when the noun is masculine, ***ma*** is used when the noun is feminine and ***mes*** is used when the noun is plural.

Note that ***mon*** is used when a feminine word begins with a vowel, to ease pronunciation:

Example

mon amie	*my (girl)friend*
mon adresse	*my address*

2 Tu comprends?
Here is Michel talking about his family. Fill in the gaps with either ***mon***, ***ma*** or ***mes***. If you don't know what a word means, look it up in a dictionary and find out if it is masculine or feminine.

«Bonjour, je m'appelle Michel. Il y a quatre personnes dans ..... famille - ..... père, ... mère, ... sœur et moi. J'ai deux cousins aussi. ..... cousins s'appellent Bill et Ben. Ils adorent les fleurs. ..... oncle s'appelle Rupert et ..... tante s'appelle Gertrude. ..... grand-parents sont australiens. Ils habitent en Australie. ..... grand-père est très sympa. ..... grand-mère est pénible!»

3 There are also three words for 'your' in French (when you use ***tu*** to address somebody): ***ton***, ***ta*** and ***tes***.

Example

ton père	*your father*
ta mère	*your mother*
tes parents	*your parents*

Note, again, that ***ton*** is masculine, ***ta*** is feminine and ***tes*** is plural, and the same rule applies (see point 1 above) when a feminine word begins with a vowel. These words can be useful for finding out information about someone else's family.

Example

Comment s'appelle ton frère?	*What is your brother called?*
Comment s'appellent tes frères?	*What are your brothers called?*
Quel âge a ta sœur?	*How old is your sister?*
Quel âge ont tes sœurs?	*How old are your sisters?*
Où habite ton père?	*Where does your father live?*
Où habitent tes parents?	*Where do your parents live?*

4 Tu comprends?

Your friend has written a letter to his penfriend in France for the first time. He asks you to check the letter for mistakes. You have to correct all of the words in bold type:

Angleterre, le 9 septembre

Salut,

Bonjour, je m'appelle David et mon professeur m'a donné **ta** adresse. Parle-moi de **ton** famille s'il te plaît:

Quel âge a **tes** père?
Quel âge a **ton** mère?
Comment s'appelle **ta** frère.
Comment s'appelle **ton** petite sœur?
Où habite **ton** sœur aînée?
Est-ce que **ton** grand-parents habitent près de chez vous?
Quel âge a **ton** grand-mère?
Parle-moi aussi de **ton** cousins.

À bientôt

David

5 There are also three words for 'his' or 'her' in French: ***son***, ***sa*** and ***ses***.

Example

son père	*his father* or *her father*
sa mère	*his mother* or *her mother*
ses parents	*his parents* or *her parents*

So, ***son*** is masculine, ***sa*** is feminine and ***ses*** is plural, and the same rule described above in point 1 applies when a feminine word begins with a vowel.

Using ***son***, ***sa*** and ***ses*** could help you to talk about someone else's family:

Mon ami s'appelle Brian. **Son** père s'appelle Alex et **sa** mère s'appelle Alice. Il a un frère et une sœur. **Son** frère s'appelle Ian et sa **sœur** s'appelle Judith.

6 Tu comprends?
Here is the reporter talking about the Queen's family.
Complete the passage with either ***son***, ***sa*** or ***ses***:

«Eh bien, elle s'appelle Elizabeth. Il y a six personnes dans ..... famille : elle, ... mari, ... fille et ..... trois fils. ..... trois fils s'appellent Charles, Andrew et Edward. ..... fille s'appelle Anne. La reine habite à Buckingham Palace avec ..... mari et ..... chiens. Elle adore les corgis!»

12 SOMMAIRE Words for 'my', 'your', 'his' or 'her'

masculine	feminine	plural	
mon père ton frère son cousin	ma mère ta sœur sa cousine	mes parents tes frères ses cousines	my your his, her

Remember that ***mon***, ***ton*** and ***son*** are also used with feminine and singular words which begin with a vowel:

mon amie, ton adresse, son école

13 Words for 'your' when using vous

1 Remember there are two words for 'you' in French: **tu** and **vous**

a You use **tu** when speaking to one person who is a member of your family or someone who you would normally call by their first name, such as a friend. You would also say **tu** to animals.
b You use **vous** when speaking to an older person or someone you do not know very well and wish to address politely. (In English you might normally address such people Mr X, Mrs X, Miss X or Ms X.) You also use **vous** when addressing a group of people.
c When using **vous**, there are two words for 'your': **votre** and **vos**.

Example

votre père	*your father*
votre mère	*your mother*
vos parents	*your parents*

So, use **votre** when the person or thing referred to is singular (one only), and **vos** when plural (more than one).

2 You wish to find out certain things about your teacher. Complete each of the questions using either **votre** or **vos** as appropriate:

a Quel âge a votre/vos père?
b Quel âge a votre/vos mère?
c Comment s'appelle votre/vos père?
d Comment s'appelle votre/vos mère?
e Où habitent votre/vos parents?
f Quel âge ont votre/vos enfants?
g Parlez-moi de votre/vos grand-parents.
h Parlez-moi aussi de votre/vos cousins.

Don't forget to check your answers!

3 Tu comprends?
Complete this letter using either **votre** or **vos**. The Smiths had a great time on a campsite in France: they thought the campsite owner's young son was very sweet and loved the swimming pool and the shop. They would like the campsite owner's family to come to England.

Angleterre, le 9 septembre

Monsieur,

Merci de ..... hospitalité à ..... camping. Nous nous sommes très bien amusés en France. ..... enfants étaient très gentils. Nous avons surtout aimé ..... petit Pierre. Il est très mignon et très poli!

Nos enfants ont surtout aimé ..... piscine et ..... petit magasin. ..... glaces sont délicieuses!

Si vous voulez passer ..... vacances en Angleterre, restez avec nous! Venez avec ..... femme et ..... deux enfants.

À bientôt

Les Smith

13 SOMMAIRE Words for 'your' when using vous

1 There are two words for 'your' when using **vous** to address somebody: **votre** and **vos**.

2 You use **votre** when the person or thing referred to is singular, and **vos** when the person or thing referred to is plural:

votre sœur	*your sister*
votre stylo	*your pen*
vos sœurs	*your sisters*
vos stylos	*your pens*

14 Words for 'our' and 'their'

1 There are two words for 'our' in French: ***notre*** and ***nos***. They follow the same rules as ***votre*** and ***vos*** (see Point 13). You will probably already be familiar with Notre Dame (Our Lady) - the name of the famous cathedral in Paris.

2 So, use ***notre*** when the person or the thing referred to is singular and ***nos*** when the person or the thing referred to is plural.

Example

notre père	*our father*
notre mère	*our mother*
nos parents	*our parents*

3 Tu comprends?

Complete the passage using either ***notre*** or ***nos***:

«..... collège s'appelle La Grande Erreur. Nous avons vingt-cinq élèves dans ..... classe. ..... professeur s'appelle Monsieur Peur. Il n'aime pas les élèves. ..... cours commencent à 8 heures. Nous arrivons au collège à huit heures et demie (ha ha!). ..... matière préférée c'est l'anglais. Nous allons passer nos vacances en Angleterre avec le collège et ..... copains. Nous prenons ..... déjeuner au collège. ..... plat préféré est le steak-frites. Nous finissons ..... cours à cinq heures. ..... parents n'aiment pas ça!»

Now check your answers!

4 There are two words for 'their': ***leur*** and ***leurs***. Like ***votre*** and ***vos***, and ***notre*** and ***nos***, you use ***leur*** when the person or thing referred to is singular and ***leurs*** when the person or thing referred to is plural.

Example

leur cousin	*their (male) cousin*
leur cousine	*their (female) cousin*
leurs cousins	*their (male plural or male and female) cousins*

5 Tu comprends?

Use either ***leur*** or ***leurs*** to complete the description of two little horrors' favourite things:

a ..... bonbons préférés sont les chewing gums.
b ..... musique préférée est très bruyante.
c ..... hobby préféré, c'est dormir.
d ..... boisson préférée, c'est le chocolat avec les grandes tartines.
e ..... nourriture préférée, c'est la confiture.
f ..... animal préféré, c'est le serpent.

14 SOMMAIRE Words for 'our' and 'their'

1 There are two words for 'our': ***notre*** and ***nos***.

2 You use ***notre*** when the person or thing referred to is singular and ***nos*** when the person or thing referred to is plural:

notre frère	*our brother*
notre maison	*our house*
nos frères	*our brothers*
nos maisons	*our houses*

3 There are two words for 'their': ***leur*** and ***leurs***.

4 You use ***leur*** when the person or thing referred to is singular and ***leurs*** when the person or thing referred to is plural:

leur tante	*their aunt*
leur voiture	*their car*
leurs tantes	*their aunts*
leurs voitures	*their cars*

15 Talking about what's going to happen

1 Victor le Voleur is going to rob a bank tomorrow. See if you can follow what he plans to do:

Il va sauter le mur.

Il va chercher le bateau.

Il va traverser le lac.

Il va entrer dans le jardin.

Il va monter sur la grille.

Il va casser la porte de la banque.

Il va voler l'argent.

2 Victor le Voleur has asked you to go with him. Write down what you are going to do. The first one has been done for you:

Je vais sauter le mur. ..... chercher le bateau. ..... traverser le lac. ..... entrer dans le jardin. ..... monter sur la grille. ..... casser la porte de la banque. ..... voler l'argent.

3 Notice that both ***je vais*** and ***il va*** come from the verb ***aller*** (to go). The verb which follows is in the infinitive: ***sauter*** (to jump), ***chercher*** (to look for), ***traverser*** (to cross), ***voler*** (to steal), and so on.

Example

je vais sauter	*I am going to jump*
il va voler	*he is going to steal*

You can use any part of the verb ***aller*** in exactly the same way:

aller		**infinitive**
je vais tu vas il va elle va on va nous allons vous allez ils vont elles vont	+	sauter chercher casser entrer monter traverser

Example

nous allons voler	*we are going to steal*
ils vont sauter	*they are going to jump*

You could, of course, use other infinitives too, in just the same way.

Example

je vais jouer	*I am going to play*
elle va danser	*she is going to dance*

When you use **aller** + an infinitive in this way, it is known as the 'Immediate Future Tense'.

4 Tu comprends?

Complete the following chart using the correct tense. Use the Immediate Future Tense (what you are going to do). The first two have been done for you. Don't forget to check your answers:

aujourd'hui (today)	*demain* (tomorrow)
a Je joue au tennis.	= Je vais jouer au tennis.
b Il regarde la télé.	= Il va regarder la télé.
c Tu manges la salade.	
d Il chante.	
e Elle arrive à l'école.	
f Nous habitons à New York.	

Of course, the infinitives do not have to be **-er** verbs.

Example

Aujourd'hui, je fais mes devoirs. ➔ Demain, je vais faire mes devoirs.
Aujourd'hui, je vends ma voiture. ➔ Demain, je vais vendre ma voiture.

Now try these:

g Je fais la vaisselle.
h Il finit ses devoirs.
i Nous vendons notre maison.
j Tu réponds à ma lettre.

15 SOMMAIRE Talking about what's going to happen

To use the Immediate Future Tense, use ***aller*** + the infinitive. This construction allows you to talk about what you are going to do. Here are some examples:

je vais jouer au tennis	*I'm going to play tennis*
tu vas faire tes devoirs	*you're going to do your homework*
il/elle va se promener	*he/she is going to go for a walk*
nous allons faire des achats	*we are going to do some shopping*
vous allez être à l'heure	*you are going to be on time*
ils/elles vont choisir un cadeau	*they are going to choose a present*

16 Linking verbs

1 If you want to talk about what you like doing, what you want to do, etc. you need a 'linking verb' followed by an infinitive. Look at the following examples:

J'aime jouer.	*I like playing.*
Je veux jouer.	*I want to play.*
Je peux jouer?	*Can I play?*
Je sais jouer.	*I know how to play.*
Je voudrais jouer.	*I would like to play.*
Je dois jouer?	*Must I play?*

So, you change the first verb and keep the second verb in its infinitive form (see Points 6 and 7 for information about infinitives), i.e. with **-er**, **-ir** or **-re** still attached to the stem of the verb.

2 Fill in the gaps in the following English and French sentences. Two of them have been done for you. Look first at the examples:

Example

J'aime chanter.	*I like singing.*
Je veux regarder la télé.	*I want to watch TV.*

a Je peux regarder la télé?	.....
b Je peux travailler?	.....
c	*Must I sing?*
d J'aime travailler.	.....
e	*I want to work.*
f	*I would like to work.*
g Je sais travailler.	.....

3 Match the following captions with the cartoons:

«Tu veux danser avec moi?» **«Je dois danser?»**
«Oui, tu dois danser.» **«Ils aiment écouter la musique.»**
«J'aime boire un coca.» **«Nous préférons manger.»**

4 Tu comprends?

Re-arrange the following sentences or part-sentences in bold type, putting the words in correct order to make sense of the passage.

«Bonjour, je m'appelle Pierre. **aller J'aime au collège**. **être voudrais Je docteur**. **dois Je travailler dur**. L'année prochaine, **vais je choisir** les sciences et les langues. Ma mère est anglaise, donc **sais je parler anglais**. **Nous aller voudrions Angleterre en** l'année prochaine. **Mon boire aime père la bière anglaise** et **mère ma voyager adore**.»

16 SOMMAIRE Linking verbs

1 When you use two verbs together, the second verb is in the infinitive:

je veux **faire**	*I want to do*
j'aime **faire**	*I like doing*
je sais **faire**	*I know how to do*

2 The same rule applies when these linking verbs are used in other tenses:

j'ai dû **partir**	*I had to leave*
j'allais **partir**	*I was going to leave*
je vais **devoir partir**	*I'm going to have to leave*

17 'This' and 'these', 'that' and 'those'

1 **Ce**, **cette** and **cet** are words which mean 'this':

Example

ce pull-over	*this pullover* (masculine singular)
cette jupe	*this skirt* (feminine singular)
cet anorak	*this anorak* (masculine, and word begins with a vowel; this exists to ease pronunciation. The same applies to a word beginning with a silent **h**.)

2 How much will each of these items in the shop window cost? Use the shop window to confirm whether a word is masculine or feminine:

a Ce livre coûte 100F. = *This book costs 100F.*
b ..... stylo coûte 1F.
c ..... bureau coûte 200F.
d ..... règle coûte 1F,50.
e ..... gomme coûte 2F.
f ..... crayon coûte 1F,20.
g ..... feutre coûte 2F,50.
h ..... trousse coûte 10F.
i ..... ordinateur coûte 2000F.
j ..... calculatrice coûte 50F.

3 **Ces** means 'these'.

Example

Ces stylos coûtent 3F.	*These pens cost 3F.*

Refer to the illustrations opposite to help you to complete the following sentences with the correct price for each set of articles. Don't forget to use **ces** to start each sentence.

a ..... trois livres coûtent ..... .
b ..... deux ordinateurs coûtent ..... .
c ..... quatre trousses coûtent ..... .
d ..... deux calculatrices coûtent ..... .
e ..... trois feutres coûtent ..... .

4 To emphasize the difference between 'this', 'that', 'these' and 'those', use ***-ci*** and ***-là***.

Example

ce pull-**ci**	*this pullover*
ce pull-**là**	*that pullover*
cette jupe-**ci**	*this skirt*
cette jupe-**là**	*that skirt*
ces chaussures-**ci**	*these shoes*
ces chaussures-**là**	*those shoes*

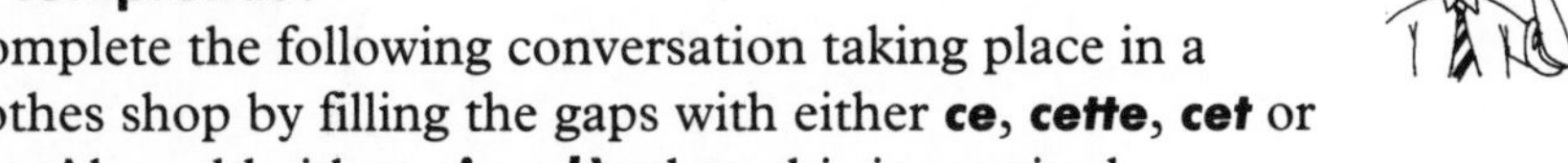

5 **Tu comprends?**

Complete the following conversation taking place in a clothes shop by filling the gaps with either **ce**, **cette**, **cet** or **ces**. Also add either ***-ci*** or ***-là*** when this is required:

- Bonjour Mademoiselle.
- Bonjour Madame. Je cherche des vêtements pour une disco ce soir.
- Et qu'est-ce que vous voulez exactement?
- Un nouveau jean, une blouse et des chaussures?
- J'ai ..... jean-ci à 250F ou ..... jean-..... à 300F.
- Je prends le noir s'il vous plaît à 300F. Qu'est-ce que vous avez comme blouses?
- Il y a ..... blouse-..... à 100F ou celle-là à 150F.
- Non merci, je prends ..... blouse-là, la bleue, à côté de ..... jupe-là.
- Et pour les chaussures, c'est décidé?
- Presque. Ou je prends ..... chaussures-..... ou celles-là. Ça y est, je prends ..... chaussures-ci à 220F.

17 SOMMAIRE 'This' and 'these', 'that' and 'those'

1 **Ce**, **cette** and **cet** are all words which mean 'this' in French.

ce pull-over (masculine)
cette jupe (feminine)
cet anorak (masculine, beginning with vowel or silent **h**)

2 The word for 'these' is **ces**:

ces chaussures	*these shoes*

3 ***-ci*** and ***-là*** are used to emphasize the difference between 'this' and 'that', and 'these' and 'those':

ce pull-**ci**	*this pullover*
ce pull-**là**	*that pullover*
cette jupe-**ci**	*this skirt*
cette jupe-**là**	*that skirt*
ces chaussures-**ci**	*these shoes*
ces chaussures-**là**	*those shoes*

18 Giving commands

1 You will have already heard your teacher giving commands. The grammatical term for language instructions which express commands is the 'imperative'.

2 How many of these can you figure out? See if you can match the French with the English. I bet you can't...!

Écoutez la cassette! **Regardez le tableau noir!**
Écrivez la date! **Lisez les instructions!** **Sortez vos affaires!**
Posez vos stylos! **Rangez vos affaires!** **Ouvrez la porte!**
Fermez la fenêtre! **Venez ici!**

Close the window! **Come here!** **Put your pens down!**
Get your things out! **Open the door!** **Write the date!**
Listen to the cassette! **Look at the blackboard!**
Read the instructions! **Put your things away!**

Make sure you check your answers.

3 Notice that ***vous*** has simply been missed off the beginning of the statement to make the command.

Example
Vous écoutez la cassette. ➔ Écoutez la cassette!

Turn the following sentences into commands:

a Vous écoutez le professeur.
b Vous regardez l'écran.
c Vous écrivez le titre.
d Vous ouvrez la fenêtre.
e Vous fermez la porte.
f Vous frappez à la porte.

Check your answers again just to make sure that you got them right.

4 If you speak to only one person, whom you address informally using ***tu***, the command is slightly different:

Tu écoutes le professeur. → Écoute le professeur!

This is the same with all regular ***-er*** verbs: take away ***tu*** and knock off the **s** from the end of the verb. Otherwise, just take the ***tu*** away.

Example
Tu viens ici → Viens ici!

Turn these statements into commands.

a Tu écoutes.
b Tu regardes.
c Tu lis le titre.
d Tu ouvres la fenêtre. (Treat ***ouvrir*** as if it were a regular ***-er*** verb.)
e Tu fermes la porte.
f Tu frappes à la porte.

Check your answers.

5 Reflexives. Sometimes you'll notice that your teacher will use **vous** or ***toi*** at the end of a command.

Example

Asseyez-vous!	Assieds-toi!	*Sit down!*
Levez-vous!	Lève-toi!	*Stand up!*
Dépêchez-vous!	Dépêche-toi!	*Hurry up!*
Taisez-vous!	Tais-toi!	*Be quiet!*

This is because they are reflexive verbs (see Point 9).

6 Tu comprends?
In each of the following instances the teacher is giving a command to either the class or to an individual. The first one has been done for you. Choose the correct command from the box opposite for each of the following:

a Teacher telling whole class to 'sit down'. = Asseyez vous!
b Teacher telling one pupil to 'come here'.
c Teacher telling one pupil to 'sit down'.
d Teacher telling whole class to 'be quiet'.
e Teacher telling whole class to 'look'.
f Teacher telling one pupil to 'look'.
g Teacher telling whole class to 'listen'.

h Teacher telling one pupil to 'stand up'.
i Teacher telling one pupil 'pack your things away'.
j Teacher telling whole class 'pack your things away'.

Levez-vous! Range tes affaires! Venez ici!
Viens ici! Taisez-vous! Écoutez! Asseyez-vous!
Regarde! Lève-toi! Rangez vos affaires!
Tais-toi! Ecoute! Assieds-toi! Regardez!

18 SOMMAIRE Giving commands

1 Tell someone to do something by removing **vous** from the beginning of the sentence:

Vous regardez.	➔	Regardez!
Vous écoutez.	➔	Écoutez!

2 When you would normally use **tu**, remove **tu** from the beginning of the sentence.

Viens ici!	*Come here!*
Choisis quelque chose!	*Choose something!*

With regular **-er** verbs, also drop the final **s** from the verb:

Tu écoutes.	➔	Écoute!
Tu regardes.	➔	Regarde!

Note
Tu vas au collège. ➔ Va au collège!

Note also the exception with **y** and **en** following the **tu** form:

Vas-y!	*Go away!*
Manges-en!	*Eat some!*

3 Remember the reflexive forms:

Asseyez-vous! or Assieds-toi!	*Sit down!*
Taisez-vous! or Tais-toi!	*Be quiet!*

4 Note the exceptions **être** and **avoir**:

Soyez sage!	*Be good!* (*vous* form)
Sois sage!	*Be good!* (*tu* form)
Ayez du courage!	*Be brave!* (*vous* form; literally, have courage)
Aie du courage!	*Be brave!* (*tu* form)

19 Au, à la, à l' and aux

1 Match up the following symbols to places in the town. You might need to look up some of the words in a dictionary:

a

b

c

d

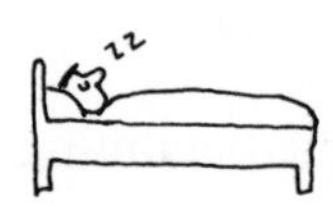

e

f

la piscine	**les toilettes**	**le cinéma**
le café	**la gare**	**l'hôtel**

2 This is where Jon is going this afternoon.

Il va à la piscine.
Il va au café.
Il va aux toilettes.
Il va au cinéma.
Il va à la gare.
Il va à l'hôtel.

Note

la piscine	→	il va à la piscine
le café	→	il va au café
l'hôtel	→	il va à l'hôtel
les toilettes	→	il va aux toilettes

Also note that only **à** is needed with place names:

Example	
Il va à Londres.	*He goes to London.*
Il va à Paris.	*He goes to Paris.*
Elles habitent à Norwich.	*They live in Norwich.*

3 Tu comprends?

This time Jon is going on a shopping spree. Complete the passage with either ***à la***, ***au***, ***à l'*** or ***aux***. Check your answers. The box below might help:

Jon adore aller ..... magasins. Pour acheter un journal, il va ..... tabac. Pour le pain, il va ..... boulangerie. Il va ..... boucherie pour la viande, et ..... pâtisserie pour des gâteaux. Pour les boîtes de conserve, il va ..... supermarché et pour les fruits, il s'arrête ..... marché. Parfois, il va ..... épicerie. Avant de rentrer ..... maison il prend un verre ..... café.

les magasins **le tabac** **la boulangerie** **la boucherie**
la pâtisserie **le supermarché** **le marché** **l'épicerie**
la maison **le café**

19 SOMMAIRE *Au, à la, à l'* and *aux*

à + la	→	à la	je suis *à la* boucherie
à + le	→	au	je suis *au* café
à + l'	→	à l'	je suis *à l'*hôtel
à + les	→	aux	je suis *aux* toilettes

20 *Du, de la, de l' and des*

1 An ***épicier*** has the following food items to sell in his ***épicerie***, or grocer's. Complete this list, in English, of what he has in his shop to sell. Use a dictionary if there are any words you do not understand.

Il a...	*He has ...*
du fromage	*some cheese*
du sucre	*some .....*
de la farine	*some .....*
de la viande	*some .....*
de l'eau minérale	*some .....*
de l'Orangina	*some .....*
des bananes	*some .....*
des œufs	*some .....*

2 ***Du***, ***de la***, ***de l'*** and ***des*** are the words for 'some':

le sucre (*the* sugar)	du sucre (*some* sugar, or simply 'sugar')
la viande (*the* meat)	de la viande (*some* meat, or simply 'meat')
l'eau (*the* water)	de l'eau (*some* water, or simply 'water')
les œufs (*the* eggs)	des œufs (*some* eggs, or simply 'eggs')

3 **Tu comprends?**

You are in a shop and you would like some of each of the following items. Complete the sentences with either ***du***, ***de la***, ***de l'*** or ***des***.

a le poulet, 20F	«Je voudrais ..... poulet, s'il vous plaît.»
b le fromage, 10F	«Je voudrais aussi ..... fromage, s'il vous plaît.»
c l'eau est à 3F	«Et avec ça, ... eau minérale, s'il vous plaît.»
d les œufs, 20F	«Avez-vous ..... œufs, s'il vous plaît?»
e la farine, 5F	«Je voudrais aussi ..... farine, s'il vous plaît.»
f Réduction sur les bananes	«Je voudrais ..... bananes.»
g le sel est à 5F	«Et avec ça ..... sel, s'il vous plaît.»
h l'Orangina est à 10F	«Je voudrais aussi ..... Orangina, s'il vous plaît.»
i la bière n'est pas chère!	«Donnez-moi ..... bière, s'il vous plaît.»
j le vrai thé anglais!	«Et je dois prendre ..... thé.»

20 SOMMAIRE *Du, de la, de l'* and *des*

1 Use ***du***, ***de la***, ***de l'*** or ***des*** for 'some'. This is known as the 'partitive article'.

2 In English, we often leave out 'some', whereas in French it is important to remember to use ***du***, ***de la***, ***de l'*** and ***des***:

Do you want tea?	*Vous voulez du thé?*
Do you want sugar?	*Vous voulez du sucre?*
Do you have jam?	*Vous avez de la confiture?*
Do you have sisters?	*Vous avez des sœurs?*

21 À côté de la banque mais en face du café

1

Note the positions of these places:

La banque est à côté du café.
Le café est à côté de la banque.
Le restaurant est à côté de l'épicerie.
La boulangerie est à côté des toilettes.

La banque est en face du restaurant.
Le café est en face de la laverie.
Le tabac est en face de l'épicerie.
La boulangerie est en face des taxis.

2 Both ***à côté de*** (next to) and ***en face de*** (opposite) are expressions containing **de** at the end. This **de** has to be changed according to what it is followed by:

Example

à côté de (le café)	➔	à côté du café
à côté de (la banque)	➔	à côté de la banque
à côté de (l'épicerie)	➔	à côté de l'épicerie
à côté de (les toilettes)	➔	à côté des toilettes

3 Tu comprends?

Use the street plan opposite to work out the positions of the following places. Complete the sentences with either ***de la***, ***du***, ***de l'*** or ***des***. Don't forget to check your answers:

a Le restaurant est en face ..... banque.
b Le restaurant est à côté ..... laverie.
c La banque est à côté ..... tabac.
d Le tabac est en face ..... épicerie.
e La boucherie est en face ..... toilettes.
f La boucherie est à côté ..... taxis.
g Les taxis sont en face ..... boulangerie.
h Les toilettes sont à côté ..... boulangerie.
i La laverie est en face ..... café.
j La boulangerie est en face ..... taxis.

21 SOMMAIRE *À côté de la banque mais en face du café*

1 Note:

à côté du café	*next to the café*
à côté de la banque	*next to the bank*
à côté de l'épicerie	*next to the grocer's*
à côté des toilettes	*next to the toilets*

2 The following expressions are used in the same way:

près de	*near*
loin de	*far from*
au coin de	*on the corner of*

3 When one of these expressions is used with, for example, the name of a chain store, there is no change:

à côté de HMV
en face de Marks and Spencers
loin de McDonald's

22 Ne... plus, ne... rien and ne... jamais

1 A reminder. The combination of **ne... pas** means 'not' (see Point 10).

Example

je **ne** joue **pas**	*I'm **not** playing, I **don't** play*
je **ne** regarde **pas**	*I'm **not** watching, I **don't** watch*

Note: the **ne** comes before the verb and the **pas** comes after the verb.

2 There are other similar constructions which are also very useful. Look at the following combination:

ne... plus	*no longer, no more*
ne... rien	*nothing*
ne... jamais	*never*

Again, in each case, a sandwich is made of the verb:

je ne chante plus	*I no longer sing*
je ne chante rien	*I don't sing anything*
je ne chante jamais	*I never sing*

3 Tu comprends?

Fill in the blanks below to complete the sentences. The first one has been done for you:

a Je ne vois rien.	*I don't see anything.*
b Je n'ai ..... de carottes.	*I don't have any more carrots.*
c Je ne parle ..... en classe.	*I never speak in class.*
d Je ne joue ..... au football.	*I no longer play football.*
e Je ne joue ..... au football .	*I never play football.*
f Je ne joue	*I don't play anything.*
g Je ne regrette	*I don't regret anything.*
h Je ..... dis	*I'm not saying anything.*
i Je ..... vais ..... au cinéma.	*I never go to the pictures.*
j Je ..... vais ..... au cinéma.	*I no longer go to the pictures.*

22 SOMMAIRE *Ne... plus, ne... rien* and *ne... jamais*

Note:

ne... plus	*no longer, no more*
ne... rien	*nothing*
ne... jamais	*never*
il ne joue plus	*he no longer plays*
il ne fait rien	*he does/makes nothing*
il ne joue jamais	*he never plays*

23 The Past Perfect Tense with regular verbs

1 The Past Perfect Tense is used to describe what happened in the past. It is used to describe an action which has been completed. Here is Michel talking about a few of the things that he did yesterday:

Hier, j'ai travaillé en classe, j'ai joué au football, j'ai écouté mes CDs et j'ai regardé la télé.

2 Notice that each action is made up of two parts:
auxiliary + past participle

auxiliary		past participle
j'ai j'ai j'ai j'ai	+	travaillé joué écouté regardé

a The auxiliary comes from the verb ***avoir***.

b The past participle of regular **-er** verbs comes from knocking the **-er** off the infinitive and adding **é**.

3 Note, therefore, that the Past Perfect of regular **-er** verbs is constructed as follows:

auxiliary (***avoir***)		past participle (**-er** → **é**)
j'ai tu as il/elle/on a nous avons vous avez ils/elles ont	+	travaillé joué écouté regardé

Example

j'ai travaillé	*I worked/I have worked*
nous avons travaillé	*we worked/we have worked*
ils ont travaillé	*they worked/they have worked*

The same structure may, of course, be applied to other regular **-er** verbs. Note, the auxiliary verb indicates who did the action, and the past participle indicates which action took place.

4 Re-write the following sentences in the Past Perfect. The first one has been done for you. Use the table opposite to help you. Don't forget to check your answers.

a Elle chante. = Elle a chanté.
b Nous regardons un bon film.
c Je discute avec mes copains.
d Tu danses?
e Vous jouez au foot?
f Il travaille en classe.
g Nous gagnons le match.
h Tu refuses?
i Il triche.
j Ils pêchent les truites.

5 The Past Perfect may also be constructedwith regular ***-ir*** verbs and regular ***-re*** verbs:

a The past participle of regular ***-ir*** verbs comes from knocking the ***-ir*** off the infinitive and adding ***i***:

Example

finir	➔	fini
choisir	➔	choisi

The past participle of regular ***-re*** verbs comes from knocking the ***-re*** off the infinitive and adding ***u***:

Example

vendre	➔	vendu
perdre	➔	perdu

So, the structure for regular verbs in the Past Perfect is as follows:

auxiliary (avoir)		past participle (-er → é)
j'ai tu as il/elle/on a nous avons vous avez ils/elles ont	+	travaillé joué fini choisi vendu perdu

6 Tu comprends?

The following story is written in the Past Perfect Tense. If you change the infinitives in brackets into the Past Perfect, the story will make sense. Make sure you check your answers.

L'amour chez les jeunes

Le travail au collège a fini à trois heures et demie. Martine (finir) ses devoirs à la maison. André (rencontrer) Martine devant le cinéma à sept heures et demie. Ils (regarder) le film ensemble. Le film était triste et les deux jeunes gens (pleurer) pendant deux heures. Après le film, ils (décider) d'aller au 'Café des Jeunes Amoureux' ensemble. Martine (choisir) un coca et Jean-Claude (préférer) un Orangina. Cinq minutes plus tard, André (commander) une bière blonde mais la serveuse (répondre):

– André, tu es trop jeune, finis ton Orangina et emmène ta copine chez elle!

Ils sont partis ensemble. Devant sa maison, Martine (embrasser) André. André était fou de joie. Les deux jeunes gens étaient amoureux!

23 SOMMAIRE The Past Perfect with regular verbs

1 The Past Perfect Tense is used to describe an action which has taken place and been completed in the past:

j'ai joué au foot	*I played football/I have played football*
j'ai regardé la télé	*I watched TV/I have watched TV*

2 The Past Perfect Tense with regular verbs is constructed as follows:

auxiliary (***avoir***)		**past participle** (**-er → é, -ir → i, -re → u**)
j'ai tu as il/elle/on a nous avons vous avez ils/elles ont	+	travaillé joué fini choisi vendu perdu

24 The Past Perfect Tense with irregular verbs

Make sure you are clear about the construction of the Past Perfect with regular verbs (Point 23) before reading this Point.

1 As you know, the Past Perfect is made up of two parts: the auxiliary verb and the past participle. The auxiliary (most frequently ***avoir***, but sometimes **être** - see Point 25) indicates who did the action, and the past participle indicates what actually happened.

2 Past participles of irregular verbs have to be learned separately. Here is a list of some of the most common irregular past participles:

auxiliary (*avoir*)		**past participle**
j'ai tu as il/elle/on a nous avons vous avez ils/elles ont	+	été (*was*) eu (*had*) pris (*took*) fait (*did/made*) dit (*said*) reçu (*received*) bu (*drank*) couru (*ran*) pu (*was able*) vu (*saw*) lu (*read*) voulu (*wanted*) offert (*offered*) ouvert (*opened*) écrit (*wrote*) mis (*put on*) compris (*understood*) appris (*learned*) dû (*had to*) dormi (*slept*) menti (*lied*)

Example

J'ai reçu une lettre.	*I have received a letter.*
Elle a bu un coca.	*She has drunk a (glass/can of) coke.*
Nous avons compris.	*We have understood.*

3 Tu comprends?

Fill in the gaps with the appropriate verbs in the Past Perfect Tense to complete the following sentences. The first one has been done for you.

a	J'ai pris mon petit déjeuner.	*I had my breakfast.*
b	Elle ..... au revoir.	*She said goodbye.*
c	J' ..... une lettre.	*I received a letter.*
d	Il ..... la tour Eiffel.	*He saw the Eiffel Tower.*
e	Nous ..... nos devoirs.	*We've done our homework.*
f	Vous ..... le journal?	*Have you read the paper?*
g	Tu .....?	*Did you understand?*
h	J'..... bien ....., merci.	*I slept well, thank you.*
i	Ils ..... partir.	*They had to leave.*
j	On ..... la vaisselle ensemble.	*We did the washing-up together.*

24 SOMMAIRE The Past Perfect with irregular verbs

1 The Past Perfect Tense with irregular verbs is constructed as follows:

auxiliary (*avoir*)		**past participle**
j'ai tu as il/elle/on a nous avons vous avez ils/elles ont	+	été (*was*) eu (*had*) pris (*took*) fait (*did/made*) dit (*said*) reçu (*received*)

2 In order to use the language with confidence you should learn the irregular past participles thoroughly. The most common ones listed in this section would give you a good start!

25 The Past Perfect Tense with être

1 Some verbs take **être** as an auxiliary in the Past Perfect Tense:

Example

je suis allé	*I have gone*
il est arrivé	*he has arrived*

There are thirteen verbs altogether which take **être**:

descendre	*to go down, to get out* (of train, car, etc.)	**s**ortir	*to go out*
retourner	*to go back, to return*	**v**enir	*to come*
aller	*to go*	**a**rriver	*to arrive*
partir	*to go away, to leave*	**n**aître	*to be born*
entrer	*to enter*	**m**onter	*to go up, to climb*
rester	*to stay*	**m**ourir	*to die*
		tomber	*to fall*

These thirteen verbs can be remembered by learning:

DRAPERS VAN MMT!

2 The structure is as follows:

auxiliary (être)		**past participle (of the above thirteen verbs)**
je suis tu es il/elle/on est nous sommes vous êtes ils/elles sont	+	descendu(es) retourné(es) allé(es) parti(es) entré(es) resté(es) sorti(es) venu(es) arrivé(es) né(es) monté(es) mort(es) tombé(es)

3 When using ***être***, the past participle also has to 'agree with' who or what did the action:

il est entré	*he entered*
elle est entré**e**	*she entered*
ils sont entré**s**	*they* (masculine plural) *entered*
elles sont entré**es**	*they* (female plural) *entered*

Note
When ***on*** refers to more than one person, agreement of the past participle is needed:

on est arrivés	*we* (here, masculine plural) *arrived*

4 Complete the sentences in the third column in the plural with the appropriate use of the Past Perfect and the necessary agreements. The first one has been done for you.

a Je suis descendu du bus.	mais	Nous sommes descendus du bus.
b Il est parti.	mais	Ils ..... .
c Elle est allée au cinéma.	mais	Elles ..... .
d Tu es parti en vitesse.	mais	Vous ..... .
e Je suis resté à la maison.	mais	Nous ..... .
f Il est monté dans le bus.	mais	Ils ..... .
g Elle est arrivée à neuf heures.	mais	Elles ..... .
h Il est mort.	mais	Ils ..... .
i Tu es né.	mais	Vous ..... .
j Je suis tombé amoureux.	mais	Nous ..... .

5 Tu comprends?
This is Chris' and Jon's school routine today:

Ils **prennent** leur petit déjeuner à sept heures et demie. Ils **quittent** la maison à huit heures pour aller à la gare. Ils **montent** dans le train à huit heures et quart. Peu après, ils **arrivent** à leur destination. Ils **descendent** du train. Ils **arrivent** au collège dix minutes plus tard. Ils **discutent** avec leurs copains dans la cour. Ils **entrent** dans la classe. À neuf heures, les cours **commencent**. Le collège **finit** à trois heures et demie.

Yesterday, their routine was exactly the same. Re-write the passage in the Past Perfect by changing the verbs that are in bold type. Use Points 23 and 24 to help you; some verbs take ***avoir*** as the auxiliary and others take ***être*** and have to agree! Don't forget to check your answers!

25 SOMMAIRE The Past Perfect Tense with être

1 There are thirteen verbs which take **être** in the Past Perfect instead of ***avoir***. These can be remembered by the mnemonic DRAPERS VAN MMT.

2 Verbs taking **être** in the Past Perfect also have to agree with who or what is doing the action:

Il est allé au cinéma.	*He went to the cinema.*
Elle est allé**e** au cinéma.	*She went to the cinema.*
Ils sont allé**s** au cinéma.	*They* (more than one male) *went to the cinema.*
Elles sont allé**es** au cinéma.	*They* (more than one female) *went to the cinema.*

3 Also note that verbs which contain one of these thirteen verbs take **être** as an auxiliary in the Past Perfect: **revenir**, **devenir**, **rentrer**, etc.

Je suis rentré un peu tard hier.	*I got back rather late yesterday.*
Nous sommes devenus très riches!	*We have become very rich!*

26 The Past Perfect Tense with reflexive verbs

1 Have another look at Point 9 to revise reflexive verbs, and also Point 25 to remind you of the use of the Past Perfect Tense with verbs which take ***être***.

2 When using the Past Perfect with reflexives, you need to remember to use the reflexive pronoun (***me***, ***te***, ***se***, ***nous***, ***vous***, ***se***) as well as ***être*** as the auxiliary. The structure is:

reflexive pronoun + auxiliary (*être*) + past participle

je me suis		réveillé(es)	*(woke up)*
tu t'es		levé(es)	*(got up)*
il/elle/on s'est		lavé(es)	*(washed)*
nous nous sommes	+	habillé(es)	*(dressed)*
vous vous êtes		rasé(es)	*(shaved)*
ils/elles se sont		couché(es)	*(went to bed)*
		promené(es)	*(went for a walk)*
		douché(es)	*(showered)*

Note also that because ***être*** is used as the auxiliary, the past participle has to agree with who or what did the action.

3 Complete the following sentences by filling in the gaps with the missing words. All of the verbs used are reflexive. Make sure you check your answers

a  Je ..... suis réveillé/e.

c  Ils se ..... habillés.

b  Elle s'est ..... .

d  Il s' ..... .

e  Elles se ..... .

f  Je ..... .

g  Tu t' .....?

h Elle ..... lavée.

4 Tu comprends?

The following passage describes you and your friend's routine as you might talk about it to someone:

Nous nous réveillons assez tôt, vers sept heures. **Nous nous habillons** et **nous nous lavons**. Vers sept heures et demie **nous prenons** le petit déjeuner - c'est d'habitude du toast avec du thé. **Nous quittons** la maison vers huit heures pour aller au collège. **Nous arrivons** au collège vers huit heures et demie. À cinq heures du soir **nous rentrons** à la maison. **Nous prenons** le dîner vers sept heures. **Nous faisons** nos devoirs et **nous nous couchons**.

By changing the verbs in bold type, use the Past Perfect Tense to describe what you did yesterday. Take your time and use the last three Points (23, 24 and 25) to help you and don't forget to check your answers!

26 SOMMAIRE The Past Perfect Tense with reflexive verbs

1 Reflexive verbs take ***être*** as the auxiliary in the Past Perfect Tense.

2 The structure is as follows:

reflexive pronoun + auxiliary (*être*) + past participle

3 Note that because reflexives take ***être*** as the auxiliary verb, the past participle must agree with who or what did the action.

27 Making comparisons and superlatives

Comparisons

1 *plus, moins, aussi*

plus	*more*
moins	*less*
aussi	*as*

Pierre est plus grand que Michel.
Michel est moins grand que Pierre.

Françoise est plus grande que Marie.
Marie est moins grande que Françoise.

Pierre est aussi grand que Françoise.
Françoise est aussi grande que Pierre.

Note that the adjectives still agree with what they are describing: notice the change in the spelling of ***grand***.

2 Comparisons can also be made with other adjectives. Complete the sentences below, using the illustrations to help you decide whether you should fill the gaps with ***plus***, ***moins*** or ***aussi***. Don't forget to check your answers:

a La France est ..... grande que l'Angleterre.

b L'Angleterre est ..... grande que l'Irlande.

c Je suis ..... riche que la reine.

d La tour de Blackpool est ..... haute que la tour Eiffel.

e Une Rolls Royce est ..... chère qu'un Mini.

f Une souris est ..... grosse qu'un éléphant.

g Pierre est ..... intelligent que Françoise.

h Marie est ..... forte que Michel.

i Michel est ..... stupide que Marie.

j Le français est ..... difficile que le chinois.

3 Tu comprends?

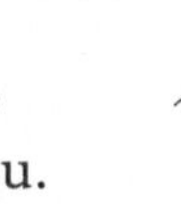

Based on the exercise above, change each of the above sentences around. The first two have been done for you. Make sure you check your answers:

a L'Angleterre est moins grande que la France.
b L'Irlande est moins grande que l'Angleterre.
c La reine ..... moi.
d La tour Eiffel ..... .
e Une Mini ..... .
f Un éléphant ..... .
g Françoise ..... .
h Michel ..... .
i Marie ..... .
j Le chinois ..... .

4 There are a few adjectives which cannot be turned into comparisons using ***plus*** as described above. It is useful to learn these special forms of comparison as they are quite common.

adjective		*comparative adjective*
bon	→	meilleur que (*better than*)
mauvais	→	pire que (*worse than*)

Example

Il est meilleur que moi.	*He is better than me.*
Elle est meilleure que moi.	*She is better than me.*
Il est pire que moi.	*He is worse than me.*
Elle est pire que moi.	*She is worse than me.*

Superlatives (the biggest, the smallest, the best, the worst, etc.)

5 a *Note:*

grand	=	*big*	plus grand	=	*bigger*	le plus grand	=	*the biggest*
petit	=	*small*	plus petit	=	*smaller*	le plus petit	=	*the smallest*
bon	=	*good*	meilleur	=	*better*	le meilleur	=	*the best*

b Note these examples:

Pierre est plus grand que Michel.
Michel est plus grand que Jean.

Pierre est le plus grand.
Jean est le moins grand.

or

Pierre est le moins petit.
Jean est le plus petit.

c Also note the following examples:

Françoise est plus grande que Marie.
Marie est plus grande que Suzanne.

Françoise est la plus grande.
Suzanne est la moins grande.

or

Françoise est la moins petite.
Suzanne est la plus petite.

6 Tu comprends?

Refer back to exercise 2 above, and use the statements to write down which is the biggest etc. The first one has been done for you. Don't forget to check your answers:

a Entre la France et l'Angleterre, la France est la plus grande.
b Entre l'Angleterre et l'Irlande, l'Angleterre ..... .
c Entre moi et la reine, je suis ..... .
d Entre la tour Eiffel et la tour de Blackpool, la tour Eiffel ..... .
e Entre une Mini et une Rolls Royce, une Mini ..... .
f Entre un éléphant et une souris, une souris ..... .
g Entre Françoise et Suzanne, Suzanne ..... .
h Entre Michel et Jean, Jean ..... .
i Entre Marie et Françoise, Françoise ..... .
j Entre le français et le chinois, le chinois ..... .

27 SOMMAIRE Making comparisons and superlatives

1 *Note:*

plus... que	*more than*
moins... que	*less than*
aussi... que	*as ... as*

La tour Eiffel est plus haute que la tour de Blackpool.
La tour de Blackpool est moins haute que la tour Eiffel.
M. Smith est aussi riche que Mme. Smith.

2 Exceptions:

meilleur que	*better than*
pire que	*worse than*

3 *Note:*

grand	*big*
plus grand	*bigger*
le plus grand	*the biggest*

La reine est la plus riche.	*The queen is the richest.*
La tour Eiffel est la plus grande.	*The Eiffel Tower is the tallest.*
Maradona était le meilleur footballer du monde.	*Maradona was the best footballer in the world.*

28 Object pronouns

1 Subject pronouns replace the subject of a verb (i.e. the person who does the action).

Example

Janine chante.	*Janine sings.* (Here, Janine is the subject of the verb 'sing'.)
Elle chante.	*She sings.* (Here, **elle** has been used to replace 'Janine'. **Elle** is called the 'subject pronoun'.)

2 Similarly, object pronouns replace the object.

I (subject) see (verb) the man (object).
Je (subject) vois (verb) l'homme (object).

Je vois l'homme.	→	Je **le** vois. (I see him.)
Je vois le chat.	→	Je **le** vois. (I see it.)
Je vois la femme.	→	Je **la** vois. (I see her.)
Je vois la fenêtre.	→	Je **la** vois. (I see it.)
Je vois les gens.	→	Je **les** vois. (I see them.)

In this context, therefore:

le	*it/him*
la	*it/her*
les	*them*

Note that the object pronouns come immediately before the verb.

Note also: change **le** or **la** to **l'** when they are positioned immediately before a verb which starts with a vowel: **je l'aime** or **je l'adore**.

3 Write each one of these sentences with an object pronoun instead. Some of them have been done for you. Don't forget to check your answers:

a Je déteste Suzanne.	Je la déteste.
b Je déteste ses parents.	.....
c Elle adore les frites.	.....
d Nous adorons le français.	.....

e Tu lis le journal?	.....
f Je mange les bonbons.	.....
g Je vais voir ma mère.	Je vais la voir. (*Note: the object pronoun is placed before the infinitive.*)
h Nous allons voir la reine.	.....
i J'ai vu Michel.	Je l'ai vu. (*Note: the object pronoun is placed before the auxiliary.*)
j J'ai aimé le film.	.....

4 *Note:*

voici	*here is*
voilà	*there is*

and

le voici	*here it is* *here he is*
la voici	*here it is* *here she is*
les voici	*here they are.*

So

le voilà	*there it is* *there he is*
la voilà	*there it is* *there she is*
les voilà	*there they are.*

5 Tu comprends?

Answer the following questions as indicated. One of them has been done for you. Make sure you check your answers:

a Tu aimes les frites?	Oui, je les aime.
b Vous voyez la reine?	Oui, je ..... .
c Tu fais tes devoirs?	Oui, ...
d Tu prends ce pantalon?	Oui, ...

Re-read point 3g above before trying the following:

e Vous allez voir le match?	Oui, je vais .... .
f Tu vas chanter la chanson?	Oui, ...

Re-read point 3i above before trying the following:

g Tu as vu le collège?	Oui, je ..... .
h Avez-vous vu le film?	Oui, nous ..... trois fois.
i Tu as pris le hot dog?	Oui, ...
j Tu as fini ton repas?	Oui, ...

6 *Lui* and *leur*

a

lui	*to him* *to her*
leur	*to them*

Example

je lui parle	*I am talking to him/her*
je lui lis	*I am reading to him/her*
je leur parle	*I am talking to them*
je leur lis	*I am reading to them*

b ***Lui*** and ***leur*** are 'indirect object pronouns' (to him, to her, to them), whereas **le**, ***la*** and **les** are 'direct object pronouns' (simply him, her, them; i.e. the preposition 'to' is absent).

Notice the difference:

je **le** vois	*I see him* (direct object pronoun)
je **lui** parle	*I speak **to** him* (indirect object pronoun)
je **les** vois	*I see them* (direct object pronoun)
je **leur** parle	*I speak **to** them* (indirect object pronoun)

c Note also that in French you say **répondre à** and **demander à**. So:

je lui réponds	*I answer him/her*
je lui demande	*I ask him/her*
je leur réponds	*I answer them*
je leur demande	*I ask them*

There are other verbs which take **à**.

7 Tu comprends?

Add the missing sentences. Some of them have been done for you:

a *I am writing to her.*	Je lui écris.
b *I am writing to them.*	.....
c	Je leur offre un cadeau.

Remember the **lui** or **leur** before the infinitive with these:

d *I'm going to see her.*	.....
e	Je vais leur parler. (*Note indirect object pronoun is positioned before the infinitive.*)

Remember to position **lui** or **leur** before the auxiliary in the Past Perfect Tense:

f	Je leur ai parlé en français.
g *I wrote to them in French.*	.....
h *I answered them.* (répondre à)	.....
i	Je leur ai demandé une glace.
j *I asked him for an ice cream.*	.....

8 Note that **me**, **te**, **nous** and **vous** are used as both direct and indirect object pronouns:

me (m')	*me/to me*
te (t')	*you/to you*
nous	*us/to us*
vous	*you/to you*

Example

je te parle	*I am speaking to you*
je te vois	*I see you*
je vais te voir	*I am going to see you*
je t'ai vu	*I saw you*

9 Tu comprends?

Complete the following sentences in French. The first one has been done for you. Note that the same rules about positioning apply with the different tenses. Check your answers:

a *I am writing to you.*	Je t'écris.
b *Are you speaking to me?*	Tu .... .
c *She loves me.*	.....
d *She hates us.*	.....
e *I am going to write to you.*	.....
f *She wrote to me.*	.....
g *He saw us.*	.....
h *Monsieur, I saw you.*	.....
i *She answered me.*	.....
j *Jean-Michel, I saw you.*	.....

28 SOMMAIRE Object pronouns

1 Direct object pronouns

je le vois	*I see him/it*
je la vois	*I see her/it*
je les vois	*I see them*

Note: for use with verbs which do not take the preposition **à**.

2 Indirect object pronouns

je lui parle	*I speak to him/her*
je leur parle	*I speak to them*

Note: for use with verbs which take the preposition **à**.

3 ***Me***, ***te***, ***nous*** and ***vous*** - direct and indirect

tu me vois	*you see me*
tu me parles	*you speak to me*
je t'aime	*I love you*
je t'écris	*I write to you*
vous nous aimez	*you love us*
vous nous écrivez	*you write to us*
je vous vois	*I see you*
je vous écris	*I write to you*

4 Position of object pronouns:

In the Present Tense, the object pronoun is usually positioned before the verb:

je **le** vois
je **lui** parle
je **te** parle

Where there are two verbs, the object pronoun should be positioned before the infinitive:

Je vais le voir.	*I am going to see him.*
Je voudrais lui parler.	*I would like to speak to him.*
Je peux vous voir?	*Can I see you?*

In the Past Perfect, the direct object comes before the auxiliary:

je **l'**ai vu	*I saw him/her*
je **lui** ai écrit	*I wrote to him/her*
je **t'**ai demandé	*I asked you*

5 Agreement of direct object pronouns in the Past Perfect:

je l'ai vu	*I saw him*
but	
je l'ai vue	*I saw her*
and	
je t'ai vu	*I saw you* (male)
or	
je t'ai vue	*I saw you* (female)
and	
je les ai vus	*I saw them*
or	
je les ai vues	*I saw them* (feminine plural)

Note: The past participle only agrees with a direct object pronoun.

je leur ai parlé	*I spoke to them* (no agreement!)

29 Ne... personne and ne... que

1 As you know already from Points 10 and 22 :

ne... pas	*not*
ne... plus	*no more/no longer*
ne... rien	*nothing*
ne... jamais	*never*

Example

je **ne** chante **pas**	*I'm not singing/I don't sing*
je **ne** chante **plus**	*I'm no longer singing/I no longer sing*
je **ne** chante **rien**	*I'm not singing anything/I don't sing anything*
je **ne** chante **jamais**	*I never sing*

2 Position of negatives:

a Both parts of the negative make a sandwich of the verb - see above.
b Where there are two verbs, both parts of the negative make a sandwich of the first verb:

Example

je **ne** vais **pas** chanter	*I am not going to sing*
je **ne** veux **plus** chanter	*I am not going to sing any longer*

c In the Past Perfect, the two parts of the negative make a sandwich of the auxiliary:

Example

je **n'**ai **pas** chanté	*I have not sung*
je **n'**ai **jamais** chanté	*I have never sung*

3 **a** *Note:*

ne... personne	*nobody/not anybody*
ne... que	*only*

Example

je **ne** vois **personne**	*I don't see anybody*
je **n'**ai **que** 6F	*I only have 6F*

b However, where there are two verbs and also in the Past Perfect, the position of ***ne... personne*** and ***ne... que*** is different from the other negative constructions:

je ne vais voir personne	(*make a sandwich of both verbs*)
je ne veux voir personne	(*make a sandwich of both verbs*)
il ne veut voir que sa femme	(*make a sandwich of both verbs*)
il n'a vu personne	(*make a sandwich of auxiliary and past participle*)
il n'a vu que trois élèves	(*make a sandwich of auxiliary and past participle*)

4 Put these jumbled up sentences into the right order. Don't forget to check your answers.

a pris / je / ai / n' / deux / que / croissants
b vu / n' / il / a / rien
c personne / vu / ai / n' / je
d regrette / rien / je / ne
e il / va / ne / personne / voir
f vu / ai / je / n' / que / personnes / trois
g aime / je / que / toi / n'
h aimons / n' / nous / personne
i n' / le facteur / livré / a / lettre / une / qu'
j compris / avons / n' / nous / jamais

5 Tu comprends?

Complete the missing sentences. Don't forget to check your answers.

a *I never watch TV.*	.....
b *I don't like anybody.*	.....
c *I only love you.*	..... toi.

Careful, remember the rules for the Past Perfect Tense:

d *I didn't play.*	Je n'ai pas joué.
e *I've never played.*	.....
f *I've only played once.*	..... une fois.
g *She didn't see anything.*	.....
h *She didn't see anybody.*	.....
i *We only saw the news.*	..... les actualités.
j *He didn't kill anybody.*	.....

29 SOMMAIRE Ne... personne and ne... que

1 Group 1:

ne... pas	*not*
ne... plus	*no more/no longer*
ne... rien	*nothing*
ne... jamais	*never*

(See also Points 10 and 22)

2 Group 2:

ne... personne	*nobody/not anybody*
ne... que	*only*

3 All negatives make a sandwich of the verb.

4 When there are two verbs following one another, the negatives of the first group make a sandwich of the first verb. The negatives of the second group make a sandwich of both verbs.

Je ne veux rien voir.	*I don't want to see anything.*
but	
Je ne veux voir personne.	*I don't want to see anybody.*

5 In the Past Perfect, the negatives of the first group make a sandwich of the auxiliary. The negatives of the second group make a sandwich of the auxiliary and the past participle.

Je n'ai rien vu.	*I saw nothing.*
but	
Je n'ai vu personne.	*I saw nobody.*

30 Venir de

1 If you wish to talk about what somebody has just done, use the expression:

***venir de* + infinitive**

2 Match the captions with the correct cartoons:

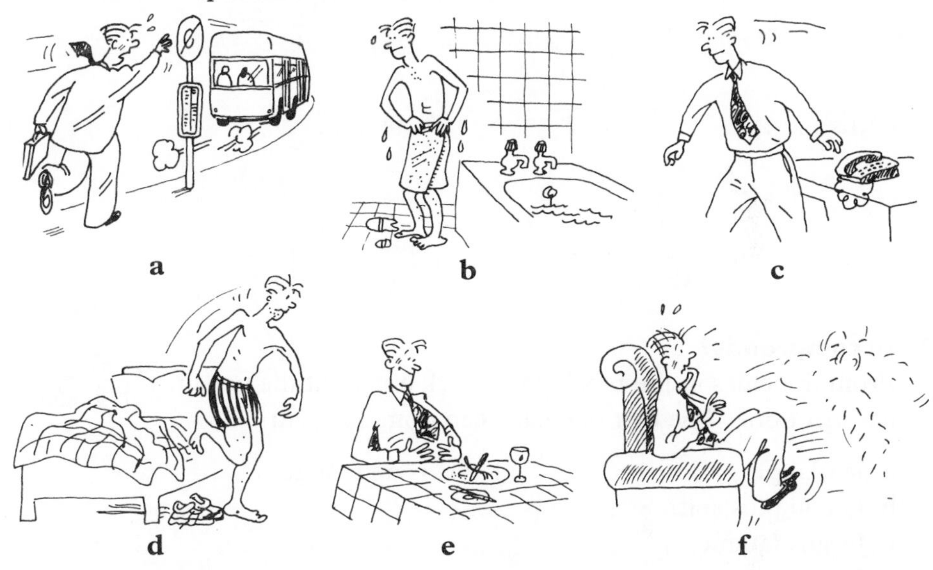

a b c d e f

Il vient de déjeuner.
Il vient de voir un fantôme.
Il vient de se lever.
Il vient de téléphoner.
Il vient de manquer son bus.
Il vient de prendre un bain.

3 Using the following structure, complete the following sentences:

Je	viens	de	manquer le bus.
Tu	viens		prendre un bain.
Il/elle/on	vient		prendre une douche.
Nous	venons		(se) lever.
Vous	venez		déjeuner.
Ils/elles	viennent		voir un fantôme.

a Je ..... .

b Nous ..... .

c Ils ..... .

d Vous ..... .

e Tu ..... .

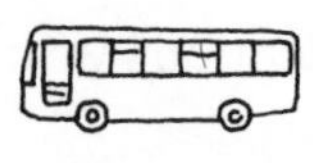

f Je ..... .

4 Tu comprends?

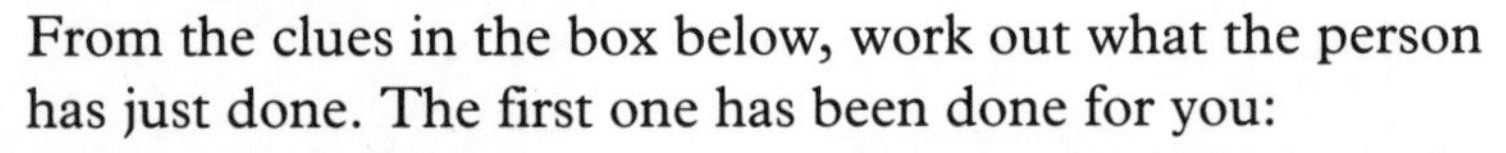

From the clues in the box below, work out what the person has just done. The first one has been done for you:

a Je n'ai plus faim. Je viens de manger.
b Je n'ai plus soif. .....
c Je suis fatigué. .....
d Je comprends. .....
e Je suis très content. .....
f Je n'ai plus froid, merci. .....
g Je suis mort. .....
h J'ai peur. .....
i J'ai mal aux dents. .....
j Je suis un bon élève. .....

Je viens de mourir. Je viens de téléphoner chez le dentiste.
Je viens de voir un fantôme. Je viens de mettre le radiateur.
Je viens de faire mes devoirs. Je viens de faire 10km à pied.
Je viens de gagner 1000F. Je viens d'acheter un dictionnaire.
Je viens de boire une limonade.

30 SOMMAIRE *Venir de*

1 The expression **venir de** + infinitive means 'to have just done something'.

Je viens de faire mes devoirs.	*I've just done my homework.*
Nous venons de nous marier.	*We've just got married.*
Ils viennent de partir.	*They've just left.*

31 Using y

1 Pour mes vacances...

... je vais en France. J'y vais avec la famille. Nous y allons en voiture.

a Notice that **y** is used to mean 'there' and that it goes before the verb.

Example

Je vais en France.	*I go to France.*
J'y vais.	*I go there.*
Nous y allons.	*We go there.*

2 Firstly, underline the word(s) in each sentence which refer(s) to the place. Then, re-write the following sentences using **y** instead of the name of the place. The first two have been done for you. Be sure to check your answers:

a Je vais en Espagne avec mes amis.
Je vais <u>en Espagne</u> avec mes amis.
J'y vais avec mes amis.
b Je vais au cinéma ce soir.
Je vais <u>au cinéma</u> ce soir.
J'y vais ce soir.
c Tu vas au match de foot avec ta correspondante?
d Vous écrivez souvent en France?
e Ils retournent à la maison.
f Il rentre en Angleterre.
g Elle reste chez elle.
h Elle va souvent à la disco.
i Elles dansent beaucoup à la disco.
j Vous allez au restaurant avec nous?

3 Now look at the difference between someone talking about what they did last year and what they are going to do next:

a In the past, **y** comes before the auxiliary.

Example

– L'année dernière j'ai pris des vacances aux États Unis. J'y suis allé avec ma copine. Il y a fait très beau. Nous y avons beaucoup nagé...

b When you talk about what is going to happen, **y** comes before the infinitive.

Example

– L'année prochaine, je vais y retourner mais cette fois je vais y aller avec toute la famille. On va y voir le Grand Canyon, Las Vegas, Disneyland... tout! Tu vas y aller avec moi?

4 Tu comprends?

Re-write this passage, using **y** instead of the place names which have been underlined. Don't forget to check the answers.

– L'année dernière j'ai pris des vacances à Paris. Je suis allé à Paris avec mes parents. Il a fait très mauvais à Paris donc nous avons passé notre temps dans les grands magasins. En plus, nous avons vu toutes les curiosités à Paris.

– Cette année je reste en Angleterre. Il fait beau en Angleterre donc je vais à la plage tous les weekends. Je joue dans l'eau à la plage avec mes amis. Tu vas souvent à la plage?

– L'année prochaine, je vais retourner à Paris mais cette fois je vais aller à Paris avec mes copains. On va voir tous les magasins de disques à Paris. Tu vas aller à Paris avec moi?

31 SOMMAIRE Use of *y*

Y can be used to mean 'there'.

j'y vais	*I go/am going there*
je vais y aller	*I'm going to go there*
j'y suis allé	*I went there*

32 Using en

1 Here is a picture of André's desk with various things on it. You're being asked how many there are of everything. Answer for him. Use **en** as in the first question to save repeating the item. Check your answers:

a Il y a un livre?	Oui, il y en a un. (*Yes, there is one.*)
b Il y a un crayon?	.....
c Combien de stylos y-a-t-il?	Il ..... .
d Combien de gommes y-a-t-il?	.....
e Combien de règles y-a-t-il?	.....
f Combien de trousses y-a-t-il?	..... une.
g Il y a un feutre?	.....
h Il y a une calculatrice?	.....

En might be translated as 'some', 'some of it' or 'some of them'. 'Some', 'some of it' and 'some of them' are often omitted in English.

2 Tu comprends?

Note that **en** goes in front of the verb. The word **en** might be heard in a shopping situation. Look at the first two examples and then complete the exercise. Check your answers:

Avez-vous de la farine?	Oui, j'en ai.
Avez-vous du sirop?	Non, je n'en ai plus.

a Avez-vous des melons?	(Oui, trois)
b Avez-vous du lait?	(Oui)
c Avez-vous des bananes?	(Non)

d Il y a du beurre? (Oui)
e Avez-vous un ananas? (Oui, deux)
f Avez-vous du sucre? (Non)
g Avez-vous de la bière? (Non)
h Avez-vous des bonbons? (Oui, beaucoup (*lots*))

32 SOMMAIRE The use of *en*

1 ***En*** used in this way can be translated as meaning 'some', 'of it' or 'of them'.

2 ***En*** is positioned before the verb:

Il y en a dix.	*There are ten (of them).*
J'en ai.	*I have some (of them).*
Vous en avez deux.	*You have two (of them).*

33 Qui and que

1 ***Qui*** and **que** are both used to link two parts of a sentence together.

a ***Qui*** relates back to the subject of the sentence: i.e. refers to the person or the thing doing the action.

Example
C'est la reine qui aime les corgis. *It's the Queen who likes corgis.*

(The ***qui*** refers back to ***la reine*** who is doing the liking; i.e. is the subject of the sentence.)

b **Que** relates back to the object of the sentence: i.e. refers to the person or the thing to whom/which the action is being done.

Ce sont les corgis que j'aime. *It's the corgis that I like.*

(The **que** refers back to **les corgis** that are being liked; i.e. is the object of the sentence.)

c **Que** is shortened to **qu'** before a vowel. **Qui** is never shortened.

2 A man is talking about his holidays in the South of France. Complete his sentences with either ***qui*** or **que**. Don't forget to check your answers:

a C'est le vin ..... j'aime le plus.
b C'est ce vin ..... est le meilleur de la région.
c Ce sont les vacances ..... j'adore.
d Ce sont les vacances ..... coûtent cher.
e Il y a la montagne ..... vous offre un peu de tout.
f C'est surtout la montagne ..... je préfère.
g En plus, il y a plage ..... n'est pas loin.
h C'est cette plage-ci ..... préfèrent mes enfants.

3 Tu comprends?
Complete the following story with either ***qui*** or **que**.

Rendez-vous au café
J'y suis arrivé. Je suis entré dans le café ..... je connais depuis longtemps. Le garçon ..... je vois chaque été était là. Il m'a vu et il a dit:

– C'est bien le cycliste ..... vient nous voir tous les ans?

Tout d'un coup, j'entends une autre voix ..... je reconnais. C'était la femme ..... j'avais rencontrée pendant mes vacances. La serveuse ..... nous connaissait était au coin de la salle peu allumée. Elle a mis un disque. On entendait une voix ..... chantait 'Te souviens-tu d'un slow? Et puis, j'entends:

– Jean-Claude, c'est bien toi ..... je vois?
– Oui, c'est moi, Claudine!

La femme ..... m'avait écrit tous les jours depuis un an était dans mes bras. C'est bien elle ..... m'a épousé!

33 SOMMAIRE *Qui* and *que*

1 **Qui** and **que** are both used to link two parts of a sentence together.

2 **Qui** relates back to the subject of the sentence and **que** relates back to the object of the sentence:

C'est le français qui m'intéresse.

Here, **qui** refers to subject of the sentence: i.e. the French is doing the interesting, it's interesting me.

C'est le français que j'aime le plus.

Que above refers to the object of the sentence: i.e. the French is being liked - this time, by me.

34 The Imperfect Tense and distinguishing it from the Past Perfect

1 When to use it. You use the Imperfect Tense in three different ways:

a To describe an action that was in the process of taking place:

Example
I was watching.
They were singing.

b When something used to be the case or happened regularly in the past:

Example
I used to go there every week./I would go there every week.
They used to visit us./They would visit us.

c When describing something in the past:

Example
The sky was blue.
The sun shone.

2 But remember, the Past Perfect Tense is used for actions which have been completed.

Bearing the above points in mind, decide for each English verb below whether you should use the Perfect or the Imperfect. Don't forget to check your answers.

"I used to enjoy (a) French but then my new French teacher came (b) and spoilt it (c) all. We would sing (d) songs or play (e) games but not any more. We used to work (f) hard but we would have a good time (g) too. Now all we do is graft. That's what it seems like anyway! In one lesson we had some fun (h). For a few lessons running my teacher wasn't (i) here. And as for this exercise, it's the worst one I've ever done! (j)."

3 How to construct the Imperfect Tense.

Take the ***nous*** form of the Present Tense of any verb except ***être*** and remove ***ons*** to find the stem of the verb:

nous regardons → regard
nous choisissons → choisiss
nous vendons → vend
nous faisons → fais

After that, simply add the following endings according to who was doing/used to do the action. The endings are always the same:

subject	**stem**	**Imperfect ending**	**Imperfect form**
je	regard	ais	je regardais
tu	regard	ais	tu regardais
il/elle/on	regard	ait	il/elle/on regardait
nous	regard	ions	nous regardions
vous	regard	iez	vous regardiez
ils/elles	regard	aient	ils/elles regardaient

4 See if you can translate the following sentences into French. Don't forget to check your answers.

a I was singing (**chanter**).
b She used to dance (**danser**).
c We used to work (**travailler**).
d It was sunny (**faire du soleil**).
e They were crying (**pleurer**).
f I was drinking (**boire**).
g She used to write (**écrire**).
h He had a headache (**avoir**).
i She was leaving (**partir**).
j He was having his lunch (**déjeuner**).

5 The stem for **être** is **ét**. Therefore:

j'étais — *I was*
tu étais — *you were*
il/elle/on était — *he/she/one was*
nous étions — *we were*
vous étiez — *you were*
ils/elles étaient — *they were*

6 There are some irregularities in the group of verbs ending **-ger** (such as ***manger***, ***nager***, ***voyager***. etc):

Example
manger (*to eat*)
je mangeais
tu mangeais
il/elle/on mangeait
nous mangions
vous mangiez
ils/elles mangeaient

7 Tu comprends?
Luc is talking about a vist to the country when he was young. Re-write the following passage, selecting the correct tense from the options given. Don't forget to check your answers.

Quand j'ai été / j'étais petit, j'allais / je suis allé au bord de la mer tous les weekends. Une fois je décidais / j'ai décidé d'aller à la campagne. Comme il a fait / il faisait beau, j'ai pris / je prenais mon maillot de bain. Quand nous arrivions / nous sommes arrivés il a plu / il pleuvait. Nous n'avons pas été / Nous n'étions pas contents. Nous avons mangé / Nous mangions dans un restaurant pas trop cher. Ça a été / C'était bien. Nous avons quitté / Nous quittions le restaurant assez tard et nous sommes arrivés / nous arrivions chez nous très fatigués.

34 SOMMAIRE The Imperfect Tense and distinguishing it from the Past Perfect

1 The Imperfect Tense is used in three different ways:

a To talk about an action that was taking place.
b To talk about something that used to be the case or happened regularly in the past.
c When describing something in the past.

2 The Past Perfect Tense is used for actions which have been completed.

3 To form the Imperfect Tense, find the stem from the ***nous*** form of the Present Tense and add the right ending. (See point 3 above.)

4 **Être** and the group of verbs whose infinitives end in **-ger** are formed differently. (See points 5 and 6 above.)

35 *Pour* + infinitive

1 When ***pour*** is used with the infinitive it means 'in order to do' something:

pour + infinitive = in order to do

Example

Je suis allé au café pour voir mes copains.	*I went to the café in order to see my friends.*

In English, we would probably just say 'I went to the café to see my friends', but the purpose 'in order to see the friend' would be implied.

2 Complete these sentences, selecting the appropriate answer from the box below. Don't forget to check your answers:

a Je suis allé ..... pour boire des cocas.
b Ils sont allés ..... pour nager.
c Elle est allée ..... pour danser.
d Nous sommes allés ..... pour nous promener un peu.
e On est allé ..... pour regarder un bon film.
f Nous sommes allés ..... pour bien manger.
g Je suis allé ..... pour demander un plan de la ville.
h Elle est allée ..... pour acheter de la viande.
i Il est allé ..... pour regarder le match.
j Je suis allé ..... pour dormir.

au restaurant **au café** **au jardin public** **à la boucherie**
au syndicat d'initiative **au lit** **au stade** **au cinéma**
à la piscine **à la disco**

3 Tu comprends?

Join the two sentences together using ***pour*** + infinitive. The first one has been done for you. Don't forget to check your answers:

a J'ai téléphoné à l'hôtel. J'ai réservé une chambre. = J'ai téléphoné à l'hôtel pour réserver une chambre.
b J'ai pris le train. Je suis allé à Londres.

c Je suis allé au jardin public. J'ai rencontré ma petite amie.
d Je suis allée à la pâtisserie. J'ai acheté un gâteau délicieux.
e Nous sommes allés à la poste. Nous avons pris des timbres.
f Nous avons passé par le parking. Nous avons laissé la voiture.
g On nous a offert du champagne. Nous avons fêté le premier de l'an.
h Nous avons passé par le port. Nous avons vu le bateau.
i Ma mère s'est arrêtée à la charcuterie. Elle a pris du saucisson.
j Je me suis arrêté. Je suis allé aux toilettes.

35 SOMMAIRE *Pour* + infinitive

When ***pour*** is used with an infinitive, it means 'in order to do' something, although we rarely say it in English:

Je suis allé au café pour voir mes copains.	*I went to the café to see my friends.*

36 *Après avoir* + past participle

1 It would be helpful to you to revise Points 23 to 26 before embarking on this Point.

2 To talk about 'after doing something' in French, use:

après avoir + past participle

3 Of course, because some verbs take ***être*** in the past and some verbs are reflexive there are, in fact, three constructions:

après avoir + past participle
après être + past participle
après (s')être + past participle
} = after doing something

Example

Après avoir quitté la maison, je suis allé à l'arrêt d'autobus.
After leaving the house, I went to the bus stop.

Après être monté dans le bus, j'ai composté mon ticket.
After getting on the bus, I stamped my ticket.

Après m'être promené un peu, je suis rentré chez moi.
After going for a short walk, I went home.

4 Complete the following sentences with the right words from the box below. Be sure to check your answers:

a Après m' ..... levé, je me suis lavé.
b Après m' ..... habillé, j'ai rangé mes affaires.
c Après ..... pris mon petit déjeuner, j'ai quitté la maison.
d ..... marché un peu, je suis arrivé au collège.
e ..... arrivé dans la cour, j'ai rencontré mes copains.
f ..... discuté pendant quelques minutes, je suis entré avec les autres.
g J'ai pris mon déjeuner à la maison ..... pendant toute la matinée.
h ..... à quatre heures, j'ai décidé de prendre un verre.

Après avoir **Après avoir** **Après avoir fini**
après avoir travaillé **être** **être** **avoir** **Après être**

5 Tu comprends?

In each case, join the two sentences together with either ***après avoir***, ***après être*** or ***après (s')être*** + past participle. Don't forget to check your answers:

Quelles vacances!

a J'ai chargé la voiture. Je me suis mis en route.
b Je suis arrivé au port. Je me suis présenté aux Passeports.
c J'ai trouvé ma cabine. J'ai dormi un peu.
d Je me suis habillé. Je suis allé à la disco.
e J'ai dansé un peu. Je me suis couché.
f Je suis descendu du bateau. J'ai pris la route pour le camping.
g J'ai dressé la tente. J'ai préparé un repas.
h Il a fait du soleil. Il a beaucoup plu.
i J'ai sauvé ma tente. J'ai chargé ma voiture.
j Je suis rentré. J'ai pris un bain.

36 SOMMAIRE *Après avoir* + past participle

1 The way to talk about 'after doing something' in French is to use the following constructions:

après avoir + past participle
après être + past participle
après (s')être + past participle

Après avoir mangé, j'ai fait la vaisselle.
After eating, I did the dishes.

Après être arrivé au théâtre, j'ai pris ma place.
After arriving at the theatre, I found my seat.

Après m'être couché, j'ai bien dormi.
After going to bed, I slept well.

2 When you use **être**, the agreement still applies:

Après être arrivés au théâtre, nous avons pris nos places.
After arriving at the theatre, we found our seats.

Après s'être lavés, ils sont descendus.
After having a wash, they came down.

37 Avant de + infinitive

1 To translate 'before doing something' in French, use the expression:

avant de + infinitive = before doing something

Example
Avant de monter dans le train, je composte mon ticket.
Before getting on the train, I stamp my ticket.

Je me lave avant de m'habiller.
I wash before getting dressed.

Avant d'entrer, je passe par la réception.
Before going in, I go to the reception.

2 Complete the story about this person's day by selecting the appropriate half of the sentences from the box below. Don't forget to check your answers:

a ..... à sept heures, avant de me lever.
b ....., je prends mon petit déjeuner.
c J'attends à l'arrêt, ...
d Je discute avec mes copains dans la cour, ...
e Je rentre chez moi ..... .
f Avant de retourner au collège, ...
g Le soir, je rentre vers quatre heures et demie, ...
h Je me lave les mains ..... .
i Avant de jouer avec mes copains ..... .
j Je mets mon pyjama ..... .
k ....., je lis jusqu'à ce que je sois fatigué.

Avant de m'endormir **avant de dîner** **avant de déjeuner**
avant de prendre le bus **avant d'aller au lit**
je fais mes devoirs **je prends mon dessert** **avant d'entrer**
Avant de quitter la maison **Je me réveille**

3 Tu comprends?

Imagine you are explaining to a French person, step by step, how to make a proper cup of tea. Emphasize at each stage what they need to do first by using the expression **avant de** + infinitive:

a Il faut remplir la bouilloire. Il faut brancher. = Il faut remplir la bouilloire avant de brancher.

b Il faut chauffer la théière. Il faut ajouter du thé.

c Il faut ajouter de l'eau bouillante. Il faut attendre trois minutes.

d Il faut mettre un peu de lait dans les tasses. Il faut verser le thé.

e Il faut ajouter du sucre si on en prend. Il faut tourner le thé dans la tasse.

f Il faut lever le petit doigt. Il faut goûter son thé.

37 SOMMAIRE *Avant de* + infinitive

To translate 'before doing something' in French, use the expression:

avant de + infinitive

Avant de quitter la maison j'ai dit au revoir.
Before leaving the house I said goodbye.

Avant d'arriver au collège, j'ai passé par le magasin.
Before getting to college, I popped into the shop.

38 The Future Tense

1 The Future Tense is used to talk about what will or shall happen:

Example

je regarderai la télé	*I will watch TV*
je chanterai	*I will sing*

2 The Future Tense is made up of two parts:

Future stem + Future endings

3 How to put verbs into the Future Tense

a For regular ***-er*** and regular ***-ir*** verbs, you use the infinitive as the stem and add the appropriate endings. With regular ***-re*** verbs, simply drop the **e** from the end of the infinitive to create the stem.

je	+	*stem*+ai
tu	+	*stem*+as
il/elle/on	+	*stem*+a
nous	+	*stem*+ons
vous	+	*stem*+ez
ils/elles	+	*stem*+ont

-er	-ir	-re
je regarder*ai*	je finir*ai*	je vendr*ai*
tu regarder*as*	tu finir*as*	tu vendr*as*
il/elle/on regarder*a*	il/elle/on finir*a*	il/elle/on vendr*a*
nous regarder*ons*	nous finir*ons*	nous vendr*ons*
vous regarder*ez*	vous finir*ez*	vous vendr*ez*
ils/elles regarder*ont*	ils/elles finir*ont*	ils/elles vendr*ont*

b Notice that the endings are the same as the Present Tense of the verb ***avoir***, apart from the ***nous*** and the ***vous*** forms. The Future Tense endings are always the same.

c Note, too, that even with many irregulars the stems are often formed from the infinitives in this way.

4 Change the verbs in the following sentences to the Future Tense. The first one has been done for you. Don't forget to check your answers:

C'est vendredi...

a	Il finit son travail à cinq heures.	= Il finira son travail à cinq heures.
b	Je finis le collège à trois heures et demie.	.....
c	Alors, je regarde la télé en attendant.	.....
d	J'arrive en ville, par le métro, à cinq heures.	.....
e	Je descends près des magasins.	.....
f	Il m'attend dans le restaurant.	.....
g	Nous choisissons nos plats préférés.	.....
h	Nous discutons en mangeant.	.....
i	Nous rentrons fatigués mais contents.	.....
j	Nous nous couchons tout de suite.	.....

... J'adore mes soirées avec papa!

5 Irregulars, of course, have to be learned separately. However, with one set of endings, only the stem has to be learned each time. This is normally done by learning the ***je*** form.

Example
For ***aller***, the future stem is:

-ir + Present Tense of ***avoir***: i.e. ***j'irai***

So:

j'ir**ai**	*I will go*
tu ir**as**	*you will go*
il/elle/on ir**a**	*he/she/one will go*
nous ir**ons**	*we will go*
vous ir**ez**	*you will go*
ils/elles ir**ont**	*they will go*

Here are some of the other common irregular future stems:

infinitive	*future*
acheter (*to buy*)	j'achèterai
avoir (*to have*)	j'aurai
être (*to be*)	je serai
faire (*to do, to make*)	je ferai
prendre (*to take*)	je prendrai

pouvoir (*to be able to*)	je pourrai
venir (*to come*)	je viendrai
voir (*to see*)	je verrai
boire (*to drink*)	je boirai
courir (*to run*)	je courrai
croire (*to believe*)	je croirai
devoir (*to have to*)	je devrai
dire (*to say, to tell*)	je dirai
partir (*to leave*)	je partirai
recevoir (*to receive*)	je recevrai
savoir (*to know*)	je saurai
vouloir (*to want*)	je voudrai

6 Tu comprends?

Here's somebody talking about his family's usual routine for a holiday. Next year, apparently, they will do exactly the same thing. Put the verbs, in bold, in the future tense, not forgetting to check your answers.

Chacun a son goût

Je **prends** mes vacances en France avec mes copains. Mes parents **vont** en Espagne. Ils **passent** leurs vacances dans un hôtel - avec salle de bains, un bar, une disco, une piscine chauffée, etc. Moi, je **fais** du camping. Nous y **allons** en autostop. Ma mère n'**aime** pas tellement ça, mais ce n'est pas cher! Mes parents **partent** en avion, bien sûr! Nous nous **amusons** tous en vacances et, en plus, ma sœur aînée **a** la tranquillité de la maison en Angleterre!

38 SOMMAIRE The Future Tense

1 The Future Tense is used to talk about what will or shall happen:

Je regarderai un bon film.	*I will watch a good film.*
Je danserai.	*I will dance.*

2 The Future Tense is made up of two parts:

The Future stem and the Future endings:

With regular ***-er*** verbs:	infinitive is the stem
With regular ***-ir*** verbs:	infinitive is the stem
With regular ***-re*** verbs:	knock **e** off infinitive for the stem
Irregulars:	irregular stems have to be learned separately

3 Endings are always the same and correspond to ***avoir*** in the Present Tense:

je travaillerai	*I will work*
tu finiras	*you will finish*
il/elle/on vendra	*he/she/one will sell*
nous ferons	*we will do/make*
vous prendrez	*you will take*
ils/elles iront	*they will go*

39 The Conditional Tense

1 You should revise Point 38 in preparation for this section.

2 The Conditional Tense is used to talk about what *would* happen:

Example
Si j'étais riche, j'achèterais une nouvelle voiture.
If I were rich, I would buy a new car.

J'ai dit que j'irais au match avec toi.
I said that I would go to the match with you.

3 The Conditional Tense is made up of two parts:

Future stem + Imperfect endings

4 Remember:

With regular **-er** verbs:	the infinitive forms the future stem
With regular **-*ir*** verbs:	the infinitive forms the future stem
With regular **-*re*** verbs:	the future stem is formed by knocking the **e** off the infinitive
Irregulars:	irregular future stems have to be learned separately

Example

je regarder**ais**	*I would watch*
je finir**ais**	*I would finish*
je descendr**ais**	*I would go down*
je fer**ais**	*I would do/make*

And the Imperfect endings are, of course:

je regarderais	*I would watch*
tu regarderais	*you would watch*
il/elle/on regarderait	*he/she/one would watch*
nous regarderions	*we would watch*
vous regarderiez	*you would watch*
ils/elles regarderaient	*they would watch*

5 ***Que ferais-tu... ?*** What would you do in the following cases? Complete the sentences by referring to the clues given in brackets. Don't forget to check your answers:

a ..... si tu avais mal aux dents? (aller chez le dentiste)
= J'irais chez le dentiste.

b ..... si tu avais mal à la tête? (prendre de l'aspirine) .....

c ..... si tu gagnais 10 000F? (acheter une moto) .....

d ..... si tu avais un jour de congé? (faire des devoirs) .....

e ..... si l'on t'offrait des vacances? (aller en Espagne) .....

f ..... si tu étais fatigué(e)? (se coucher) .....

g ..... si tu avais faim? (manger) .....

h ..... si tu avais soif? (boire) .....

i ..... si tu étais sale? (prendre un bain) .....

j ..... si tu avais froid? (mettre un manteau) .....

6 Tu comprends?

The Conditional Tense is also commonly used for reported speech.

Example

Il a dit «Je le ferai samedi». = Il a dit qu'il le ferait samedi.

Try these and then check your answers:

a Elle a promis «Je le ferai demain».
b Il a dit «Je téléphonerai la semaine prochaine».
c Ils m'ont dit «Nous irons au match».
d Elle m'a dit «Je t'achèterai un nouveau blouson».
e Tu m'as dit «Je n'y travaillerai plus».
f Elle m'a répondu «Je ne me lèverai jamais».
g J'ai dit au prof «Je refuserai de le faire».
h Le Premier Ministre nous a dit «Je vous dirai toujours la vérité».
i Elle a dit «Je verrai le docteur demain».
j Elles ont dit «Nous nous réveillerons de bonne heure».

39 SOMMAIRE The Conditional Tense

1 The Conditional Tense is used to talk about what would happen:

Si j'étais riche, je prendrais de longues vacances.
If I were rich, I would take long holidays.

J'ai dit que j'irais au café avec toi.
I said that I would go to the café with you.

2 The Conditional Tense is made up of two parts:

Future stem + Imperfect endings

40 An Introduction to the Subjunctive

1 It is hoped that this section will enable you to use some Subjunctive structures confidently with certain set expressions that are followed by ***que***. For a more thorough understanding of the Subjunctive, you should be considering advanced level study.

2 Structure. To form the stem, take ***ent*** off the third person plural form of the Present Tense and add the subjunctive endings.

The Subjunctive endings are:

subject	verb ending
je tu il/elle/on nous vous ils/elles	e es e ions iez ent

Example

ils finiss___ ➔ je finisse
ils mett___ ➔ nous mettions

je finiss**e**
tu finiss**es**
il/elle/on finiss**e**
nous finiss**ions**
vous finiss**iez**
ils/elles finiss**ent**

3 Irregulars. Here are the main ones:

aller: aille, ailles, aille, allions, alliez, aillent
avoir: aie, aies, ait, ayons, ayez, aient
être: sois, sois, soit, soyons, soyez, soient
faire: fasse, fasses, fasse, fassions, fassiez, fassent
prendre: prenne, prennes, prenne, prenions, preniez, prennent
pouvoir: puisse, puisses, puisse, puissions, puissiez, puissent
savoir: sache, saches, sache, sachions, sachiez, sachent
vouloir: veuille, veuilles, veuille, voulions, vouliez, veuillent

4 The Subjunctive after set expressions. There are several set expressions which require the Subjunctive to be used after them. Here are two of the most common.

bien que — *although*

Bien qu'il fasse mauvais, je vais sortir.
Although the weather's bad, I'm going to go out.

à condition que — *provided that*

À condition que je prenne le bus, je vais y arriver.
Provided I catch the bus, I'll get there.

5 Tu comprends?
The first ones each time have been done for you.

Re-write the following sentences, starting each sentence **bien que**. The first one has been done for you.

a Je suis jeune mais je suis intelligent. = Bien que je sois jeune, je suis intelligent.
b Je suis jeune mais je suis sensible.
c J'ai mal à la tête mais j'y vais quand même.
d Je fais mes devoirs mais je n'apprends rien.
e Je sais le faire mais je ne veux pas jouer!
f Je t'écris mais je ne t'aime plus.

6 Use the expression ***à condition que*** to re-write these sentences. The first one has been done for you.

a Si je travaille, je réussirai. = À condition que je travaille, je réussirai.
b Si je fais mes devoirs, je réussirai.
c Si je me couche tard, je serai fatigué.
d S'il y va, il sera content.
e Si nous finissons à l'heure, nous viendrons.
f S'il est sage, il pourra venir.

7 The Subjunctive after expressions of necessity and possibility.

Example

il faut que	*must*
Il faut que je parte.	*I must leave.*
il est possible que	*possible*
Il est possible que j'aie tort.	*I might be wrong.*

8 Tu comprends?

Your parents have a list of certain things that you have to do every evening before you can go out. Re-write the sentences, using the expression ***il faut que***:

a Tu dois promener le chien. = Il faut que tu promènes le chien!
b Tu dois ranger ta chambre.
c Tu dois faire tes devoirs.
d Tu dois prendre ton dîner.
e Tu dois débarrasser la table.
f Tu dois te laver.

9 Tu comprends?

In an interview with your careers' officer, you are talking about the various things you might do when you leave school. Use the expression ***il est possible que*** each time to express yourself:

a Je vais, peut-être, être chômeur. = Il est possible que je sois chômeur.
b Je vais, peut-être, me marier.
c Nous aurons, peut-être, des enfants.
d Nous irons, peut-être, à l'étranger.
e Nous serons, peut-être, patrons.
f Tu rêves, peut-être?

10 The Subjunctive to express desire.

Example

je veux que	*I want*
Je veux que tu viennes.	*I want you to come.*

11 Tu comprends?

Your friend in France is planning to come and stay with you. You are happy for her to do so as long as she does certain things. These things you emphasize in a letter. Use the expression ***je veux que*** to indicate what you want her to do:

– Apporter tes cassettes préférées. = Je veux que tu apportes tes cassettes préférées.

a M'écrire pour confirmer que tu viens.
b Porter ton blouson rouge pour t'identifier.
c Apporter du vin pour papa.
d Être à l'heure.

e Aller au Bureau de Change devant quai numéro 6.
f Me parler doucement en français.
g Prendre tous tes repas avec nous.
h Arrêter de fumer en Angleterre.

40 SOMMAIRE An Introduction to the Subjunctive

1 Use. The Subjunctive is used after certain set expressions. This section has focused on the following:

a Bienque, à condition que, etc.

bien que — *although*
(**quoique** means the same and can be used in the same way)

à condition que — *provided that*
(**pourvu que** means the same and can be used in the same way, but it is less common)

b Expressions of necessity and possibility:

il faut que — *must*
(***il est nécessaire que*** means the same and can be used in the same way)

il est possible que — *possible*
(***il se peut que*** means the same and can be used in the same way)

c Expressions of wish and desire

je veux que — *want*
(***je désire que*** and ***je souhaite que*** can also be used in the same way)

2 Structure. In most cases, the stem is provided by the third person plural of the Present Tense:

third person plural form of Present Tense + Subjunctive ending

Example
ils choisissent ➔ je choisisse
ils vendent ➔ je vende

je choisiss**e**
tu choisiss**es**
il/elle/on choisiss**e**
nous choisiss**ions**
vous choisiss**iez**
ils/elles choisiss**ent**

3 There are, of course, irregulars which have to be learned separately (see point 3 above).

41 An Introduction to the Past Historic

1 The Past Historic Tense is used in formal written French and, like the Past Perfect Tense, it is used to describe a completed action.

2 Structure:

a All **-er** verbs follow this pattern. Knock off the **-er** from the infinitive and add the following endings:

j'all**ai**	*I went*
tu all**as**	*you went*
il/elle/on all**a**	*he/she/one went*
nous all**âmes**	*we went*
vous all**âtes**	*you went*
ils/elles all**èrent**	*they went*

b Most regular **-ir** and **-re** verbs follow this pattern. Knock off the **-ir** or **-re** from the infinitive and add the following endings:

je fin**is**	*I finished*
tu fin**is**	*you finished*
il/elle/on fin**it**	*he/she/one finished*
nous fin**îmes**	*we finished*
vous fin**îtes**	*you finished*
ils/elles fin**irent**	*they finished*

c Many irregular verbs follow this pattern:

je voul**us**	*I wanted*
tu voul**us**	*you wanted*
il/elle/on voul**ut**	*he/she wanted*
nous voul**ûmes**	*we wanted*
vous voul**ûtes**	*you wanted*
ils/elles voul**urent**	*they wanted*

d As is the case with the last verb, there is often a similarity with the past participle. Once you have identified into which of the above three categories a verb falls, the patterns can be easily followed.

infinitive	Past historic
prendre (*to take*)	il prit
croire (*to believe*)	il crut
dire (*to say, to tell*)	il dit
mettre (*to put*)	il mit
rire (*to laugh*)	il rit
avoir (*to have*)	il eut
boire (*to drink*)	il but
connaître (*to know*)	il connut
devoir (*to have to*)	il dut
lire (*to read*)	il lut
pouvoir (*to be able to*)	il put
recevoir (*to receive*)	il reçut
savoir (*to know*)	il sut
vivre (*to live*)	il vécut

e There are, of course, irregularities which need to be learned separately, such as:

infinitive	Past Historic
conduire (*to drive*)	il conduisit
construire (*to construct*)	il construisit
écrire (*to write*)	il écrivit
faire (*to do, make*)	il fit
naître (*to be born*)	il naquit
voir (*to see*)	il vit
être (*to be*)	il fut
mourir (*to die*)	il mourut

f In addition, there is the ***venir/tenir*** pattern:

je vins	je tins
tu vins	tu tins
il/elle/on vint	il/elle/on tint
nous vînmes	nous tînmes
vous vîntes	vous tîntes
ils/elles/vinrent	ils/elles tinrent

3 Put the following sentences into the Past Historic. The first one has been done for you:

First structure:

a Elle écoute un disque. = Elle écouta un disque.
b Il regarde un bon film.
c Nous rentrons tard.

Second structure:

d Ils choisissent un livre.
e Nous finissons notre travail.

And others:

f Je bois un coca.
g Ils font leur travail.
h Je vois la tour Eiffel.
i Il vient à pied.
j Elle sort.

4 Tu comprends?

The following story should be written in the Past Historic. Change the infinitives in brackets to make it make sense. Be sure to check your answers.

Pierre (se lever) de bonne heure. Il (quitter) la maison après avoir pris son petit déjeuner. Il devait rencontrer Monique pour la première fois devant le Café de la Ville. Il (devoir) passer aux magasins d'abord. Il (aller) à la boucherie pour acheter le poulet. Ensuite, il (passer) par la boulangerie. Il (se précipiter) vers la gare. Il (prendre) le bus. Malheureusement, il y avait de la circulation. Il (regarder) sa montre. Tout d'un coup, le bus (s'arrêter). Voilà, elle était là. Ils (s'embrasser). Ils s'écrivaient depuis six ans.

41 SOMMAIRE An Introduction to the Past Historic

1 The Past Historic Tense is used in formal written French and, like the Past Perfect Tense, it is used to describe a completed action. It is never used in speech.

2 Structure.

a All **-er** verbs follow the pattern:

infinitive without **-er** + Past Historic ending: ***ai***, ***as***, ***a***, ***âmes***, ***âtes***, ***èrent***

b Most regular **-ir** and **-re** verbs follow the pattern:

infinitive without **-ir** or **-re** + Past Historic ending: ***is***, ***is***, ***it***, ***îmes***, ***îtes***, ***irent***

c Many irregulars follow the pattern:

infinitive stem + Past Historic endings: ***us***, ***us***, ***ut***, ***ûmes***, ***ûtes***, ***urent***

d There is often a similarity between the Past Historic and the past participle:

past participle	Past Historic
cru pris	il crut il prit

e ***Venir*** and ***tenir*** base fall into an separate pattern (see point 2f on page 112).

f As is often the case, there are exceptions that don't follow any rule and these, of course, have to be learned separately.

Answer section

Point 1 Using *le* and *la*

1

masculine words	*feminine words*
le parking	la boulangerie
le supermarché	la gare
le restaurant	la poste
le parc	la piscine
le camping	la banque

4 Tu comprends?

a café (**nm**)	= le café	= *the café*
b camping (**nm**)	= le camping	= *the campsite*
c piscine (**nf**)	= la piscine	= *the swimming pool*
d collège (**nm**)	= le collège	= *the school*
e port (**nm**)	= le port	= *the harbour*
f boucherie (**nf**)	= la boucherie	= *the butcher's*
g cinéma (**nm**)	= le cinéma	= *the cinema*
h église (**nf**)	= l'église	= *the church*
i tabac (**nm**)	= le tabac	= *the tobacconist's*
j hôtel (**nm**)	= l'hôtel	= *the hotel*

Point 2 Using *un* and *une*

1

masculine words	*feminine words*
un T-shirt	une chemise
un blouson	une chaussette
un soutien-gorge	une chaussure
un anorak	une cravate
un jean	une blouse

3 Tu comprends?

a soutien-gorge (**nm**)	= un soutien-gorge	= *a bra*
b pantalon (**nm**)	= un pantalon	= *a pair of trousers*
c jupe (**nf**)	= une jupe	= *a skirt*
d chapeau (**nm**)	= un chapeau	= *a hat*
e manteau (**nm**)	= un manteau	= *a coat*
f robe (**nf**)	= une robe	= *a dress*
g anorak (**nm**)	= un anorak	= *an anorak*

h ceinture (***nf***) = une ceinture = *a belt*
i short (***nm***) = un short = *a pair of shorts*
j survêtement (***nm***) = un survêtement = *a tracksuit*

Point 3 Using *les* and *des*

2 **a** *some rulers* = des règles
b *the rulers* = les règles
c *the rubbers* = les gommes
d *some pencils* = des crayons
e *the textbooks* = les livres
f *some cassettes* = des cassettes
g *the disks* = les disquettes
h *some felt-tips* = des feutres
i *the exercise books* = les cahiers
j *the tape recorders* = les magnétophones

3 Tu comprends?
a Où sont les toilettes?
b Est-ce qu'il y a un café près d'ici?
c Je vais à l'hôpital.
d Où est le cinéma?
e Il y a des taxis en face de la gare.
f Est-ce qu'il y a une boulangerie en ville?
g La poste est à deux minutes d'ici.
h J'aime beaucoup le marché en ville.
i Où est la boucherie?
j S'il vous plaît, il y a un téléphone ici?

Point 4 Adjectives

2 **a** J'ai un éléphant. Il s'appelle Pierre. Il est très grand et très gros. De couleur, il est gris.
b Voici ma voiture noire et blanche. Elle est superbe. Elle est très grande. Elle est aussi très confortable.
c Jai une souris. Elle s'appelle Sauvage. Elle est petite, blanche et méchante. Elle attaque les éléphants.

4 Tu comprends?
Je m'appelle Dylan. Je suis grand. Je suis mince. J'ai les cheveux longs et blonds. J'ai les yeux bleus. J'ai un visage long. Voici mon lapin. Il s'appelle Jake. Il est petit. Il est blanc. Il est végétarien. Il est mignon. Il est un peu gros. Il adore les carottes.

Point 5 Understanding what a verb is

2 Elle chante à l'opéra. (a) — *She's singing at the opera.*
Ils jouent au tennis. (b) — *They're playing tennis.*
Il écoute la radio. (c) — *He is listening to the radio.*
Ils dansent un slow. (d) — *They're dancing a 'slow'.*
Elle mange du fromage. (e) — *She's eating some cheese.*

4

je	=	*I*
tu	=	*you*
il	=	*he*
elle	=	*she*
nous	=	*we*
vous	=	*you*
ils	=	*they* (female plural)
elles	=	*they* (male plural)

5 Tu comprends?
Il joue au tennis. (a)
Elle joue au tennis. (b)
Ils jouent au tennis. (c)
Elles jouent au tennis. (d)
Je joue au tennis. (e)
Nous jouons au tennis. (f)
Tu joues au tennis? (g)
Vous jouez au tennis? (h)

Point 6 Using regular -er verbs in the Present Tense

3 **a** Nous écoutons de la musique.
b J'aime la musique.
c Tu danses?
d Pierre travaille dans le jardin.
e Elle regarde la télé.
f Ils restent à la maison.
g Vous parlez français?
h Elles jouent au tennis.
i Ma mère et moi écoutons la radio.
j Monique travaille au collège.

4 Tu comprends?
J'aime les samedis. Mes amis arrivent à la maison à dix heures. Nous regardons la télévision pendant trois heures. À une

heure je prends un hamburger-frites. L'après-midi je vais à la pêche avec mes copains. Nous pêchons les truites. Mon père reste à la maison. Il écoute la radio et il chante avec ses disques préférés. Ma mère danse. Elle adore danser. Le soir, je regarde un bon film à la télé. J'entre dans ma chambre vers dix heures, j'écoute la radio et je m'endors.....zzzz!

Point 7 Using regular *-ir* and *-re* verbs in the Present Tense

3 je choisis un disque
il vomit
nous rougissons
vous finissez
ils obéissent
tu perds tes devoirs
elle répond à ma lettre
nous attendons un bus
vous vendez la maison
elles répondent en français

4 Tu comprends?
C'est vendredi vingt-quatre décembre. Je m'appelle Jean Saitro. Je suis cool. J'arrive à la disco avec mes copains. Il y a une jeune fille qui danse. Elle s'appelle Céline Bisou. Elle est magnifique. Céline danse et moi, je parle avec mes copains. Elle adore danser. Plus tard, je choisis un disque pour Céline. Elle est très contente. Nous dansons le slow ensemble. Je rougis. La disco finit vers onze heures. Nous rentrons à mobylette ensemble. Mes copains attendent le bus. Je suis amoureux.

Point 8 Using irregular verbs in the Present Tense

3 **a** Il est au cinéma.
b Nous sommes à la piscine.
c Ils sont au café.
d Elle est au restaurant.
e Elles sont aux toilettes.
f Je suis à la gare.
g Vous êtes au pub.
h Tu es au match de foot?
i Je suis à Paris.
j Ils sont en France.

4 **a** Il a un ordinateur.
b Nous avons des biscuits.
c Ils ont des bonbons.
d Elle a un chien.
e Elles ont des chips.
f J'ai une perruche.
g Vous avez des bananes.
h Tu as une bicyclette?
i J'ai des devoirs.
j Ils ont des oignons.

5 **a** Il va au cinéma.
b Nous allons à la piscine.
c Ils vont au café.
d Elle va au restaurant.
e Elles vont aux toilettes.
f Je vais à la gare.
g Vous ..... allez au musée.
h Tu vas au match de foot?
i Je vais à Paris.
j Ils vont en France.

6 **a** Je prends mon petit déjeuner.
b Nous prenons le train.
c Elle prend une douche.
d Vous prenez un café?
e Tu prends le bus?
f Ils prennent le taxi.

7 je fais
tu fais
il fait
elle fait
on fait
nous faisons
vous faites
ils font
elles font

8 **Tu comprends?**
Je me réveille à sept heures. Je prends une douche et je prends mon petit déjeuner. J'adore les croissants! Je vais au collège avec mon correspondant. Nous attendons le bus. Les cours commencent à 8 heures. Je suis très fatigué. Nous prenons le déjeuner à midi. À cinq heures, les cours finissent et nous quittons le collège. À la maison, nous faisons nos devoirs. Nous faisons la vaisselle après le dîner. Je vais au lit vers dix heures.

Point 9 Using reflexive verbs in the Present Tense

4 **a** je me lave
b ils se lavent
c tu te réveilles à huit heures
d elle se lève à sept heures
e il s'habille à sept heures
f elle se promène à neuf heures
g je me couche à neuf heures et demie
h nous nous réveillons à six heures
i il se rase à sept heures et demie
j vous vous couchez à dix heures?

5 Tu comprends?

a Je me lève à sept heures.
b Ils se réveillent à six heures.
c Vous vous rasez à huit heures.
d Nous nous habillons à sept heures dix.
e Tu te promènes à sept heures et quart.
f Elle se couche à dix heures.
g Il se lave à sept heures.
h On se lève à six heures et demie.
i Nous nous promenons à trois heures.
j Ils se couchent à minuit.

Point 10 Using *ne... pas*

2 a Je ne joue pas au football.
b Elle ne regarde pas la télé.
c Nous n'écoutons pas la radio.
d Il ne danse pas à la disco.
e Ne reste pas à la maison!
f Je ne parle pas français.
g Ne prenez pas le bus!
h Je n'aime pas les sciences.
i Tu ne comprends pas?
j Vous n'aimez pas les frites?

3 Tu comprends?

a Elle aime le steak et le poulet.
b Elle n'aime pas le fromage et elle n'aime pas les œufs.
c Elle ne va pas au cinéma.
d Elle joue au ping-pong.
e Elle écoute des disques.
f Elle ne fait pas la vaisselle.
g Elle danse.
h Elle ne regarde pas la télé.

Point 11 Asking questions

2 a Il habite en France.
b Elle joue au football.
c Il parle français.
d Tu aimes la glace au chocolat.
e Tu habites en Angleterre.

f Elle aime le collège.
g Tu fais tes devoirs.
h Vous aimez le français.
i Tu as été en France.
j Tu as choisi.

4 Tu comprends?

La journaliste

a Comment vous appelez-vous?
b Où habitez-vous exactement?
c Combien d'enfants avez-vous?
d Qui est le plus âgé?
e Quand allez-vous en vacances?
f Avec qui?
g Quelle est la date de votre voyage?
h Où allez-vous?
i Pourquoi?

Point 12 Words for 'my', 'your', 'his' or 'her'

2 Tu comprends?

«Bonjour, je m'appelle Michel. Il y a quatre personnes dans ma famille - mon père, ma mère, ma sœur et moi. J'ai deux cousins aussi. Mes cousins s'appellent Bill et Ben. Ils adorent les fleurs. Mon oncle s'appelle Rupert et ma tante s'appelle Gertrude. Mes grand-parents sont australiens. Ils habitent en Australie. Mon grand-père est très sympa. Ma grand-mère est pénible.»

4 Tu comprends?

Angleterre, le 9 septembre

Salut,

Bonjour, je m'appelle David et mon professeur m'a donné ton adresse. Parle-moi de ta famille s'il te plaît:

Quel âge a ton père?
Quel âge a ta mère?
Comment s'appelle ton frère.
Comment s'appelle ta petite sœur?
Où habite ta sœur aînée?
Est-ce que tes grand-parents habitent près de chez vous?
Quel âge a ta grand-mère?
Parle-moi aussi de tes cousins.

À bientôt

David

6 Tu comprends?

«Eh bien, elle s'appelle Elizabeth. Il y a six personnes dans sa famille: elle, son mari, sa fille et ses trois fils. Ses trois fils s'appellent Charles, Andrew et Edward. Sa fille s'appelle Anne. La reine habite à Buckingham Palace avec son mari et ses chiens. Elle adore les corgis.»

Point 13 Words for 'your' when using *vous*

2 **a** Quel âge a votre père?
b Quel âge a votre mère?
c Comment s'appelle votre père?
d Comment s'appelle votre mère?
e Où habitent vos parents?
f Quel âge ont vos enfants?
g Parlez-moi de vos grand-parents.
h Parlez-moi aussi de vos cousins.

3 Tu comprends?

Angleterre, le 9 septembre

Monsieur,

Merci de votre hospitalité à votre camping. Nous nous sommes très bien amusés en France. Vos enfants étaient très gentils. Nous avons surtout aimé votre petit Pierre. Il est très mignon et très poli!

Nos enfants ont surtout aimé votre piscine et votre petit magasin. Vos glaces sont délicieuses!

Si vous voulez passer vos vacances en Angleterre, restez avec nous. Venez avec votre femme et vos deux enfants.

À bientôt

Les Smith

Point 14 Words for 'our' and 'their'

3 Tu comprends?

«Notre collège s'appelle La Grande Erreur. Nous avons vingt-cinq élèves dans notre classe. Notre professeur s'appelle Monsieur Peur. Il n'aime pas les élèves. Nos cours commencent à 8 heures. Nous arrivons au collège à huit heures et demie (ha ha!). Notre matière préférée c'est l'anglais. Nous allons passer nos vacances en Angleterre avec le collège et nos copains. Nous prenons notre déjeuner au collège. Notre plat préféré est le steak-frites. Nous finissons nos cours à cinq heures. Nos parents n'aiment pas ça!»

5 Tu comprends?

a Leurs bonbons préférés sont les chewing gums.
b Leur musique préférée est très bruyante.
c Leur hobby préféré, c'est dormir.
d Leur boisson préférée, c'est le chocolat avec les grandes tartines.
e Leur nourriture préférée, c'est la confiture.
f Leur animal préféré, c'est le serpent.

Point 15 Talking about what's going to happen

2 Je vais sauter le mur. Je vais chercher le bateau. Je vais traverser le lac. Je vais entrer dans le jardin. Je vais monter sur la grille. Je vais casser la porte de la banque. Je vais voler l'argent.

4 Tu comprends?

aujourd'hui (today)	*demain* (tomorrow)
a Je joue au tennis.	= Je vais jouer au tennis.
b Il regarde la télé.	= Il va regarder la télé.
c Tu manges la salade.	= Tu vas manger la salade.
d Il chante.	= Il va chanter.
e Elle arrive à l'école.	= Elle va arriver à l'école.
f Nous habitons à New York.	= Nous allons habiter à New York.
g Je fais la vaisselle.	= Je vais faire la vaisselle.
h Il finit ses devoirs.	= Il va finir ses devoirs.
i Nous vendons notre maison.	= Nous allons vendre notre maison.
j Tu réponds à ma lettre.	= Tu vas répondre à ma lettre.

Point 16 Linking verbs

2

a Je peux regarder la télé?	*Can I watch TV?*
b Je peux travailler?	*Can I work?*
c Je dois chanter?	*Must I sing?*
d J'aime travailler.	*I like working.*
e Je veux travailler.	*I want to work.*
f Je voudrais travailler.	*I would like to work.*
g Je sais travailler.	*I know how to work.*

(You might, of course, have chosen other question forms)

3 «Tu veux danser avec moi?» (b)
«Je dois danser?» (d)
«Oui, tu dois danser.» (e)
«Ils aiment écouter la musique.» (c)
«J'aime boire un coca.» (a)
«Nous préférons manger.» (f)

4 Tu comprends?

«Bonjour, je m'appelle Pierre. J'aime aller au collège. Je voudrais être docteur. Je dois travailler dur. L'année prochaine, je vais choisir les sciences et les langues. Ma mère est anglaise, donc je sais parler anglais. Nous voudrions aller en Angleterre l'année prochaine. Mon père aime boire la bière anglaise et ma mère adore voyager.»

Point 17 'This' and 'these, 'that' and 'those'

2 **a** Ce livre coûte 100F.
b Ce stylo coûte 1F.
c Ce bureau coûte 200F.
d Cette règle coûte 1F,50.
e Cette gomme coûte 2F.
f Ce crayon coûte 1F,20.
g Ce feutre coûte 2F,50.
h Cette trousse coûte 10F.
i Cet ordinateur coûte 2000F.
j Cette calculatrice coûte 50F.

3 **a** Ces trois livres coûtent 300F.
b Ces deux ordinateurs coûtent 4000F.
c Ces quatre trousses coûtent 40F.
d Ces deux calculatrices coûtent 100F.
e Ces trois feutres coûtent 7F,50.

5 **Tu comprends?**

– Bonjour Mademoiselle.
– Bonjour Madame. Je cherche des vêtements pour une disco ce soir.
– Et qu'est-ce que vous voulez exactement?
– Un nouveau jean, une blouse et des chaussures?
– J'ai ce jean-ci à 250F ou ce jean-là à 300F.
– Je prends le noir s'il vous plait à 300F. Qu'est-ce que vous avez comme blouses?
– Il y a cette blouse-ci à 100F ou celle-là à 150F.
– Non merci, je prends cette blouse-là, la bleue, à côté de cette jupe-là.
– Et pour les chaussures, c'est décidé?
– Presque. Ou je prends ces chaussures-ci ou celles-là. Ça y est, je prends ces chaussures-ci à 220F.

Point 18 Giving commands

2

Écoutez la cassette!	*Listen to the cassette!*
Regardez le tableau noir!	*Look at the blackboard!*
Écrivez la date!	*Write the date!*
Lisez les instructions!	*Read the instructions!*
Sortez vos affaires!	*Get your things out!*
Posez vos stylos!	*Put your pens down!*
Rangez vos affaires!	*Put your things away!*

Ouvrez la porte! — *Open the door!*
Fermez la fenêtre! — *Close the window!*
Venez ici! — *Come here!*

3 **a** Écoutez le professeur!
b Regardez l'écran!
c Écrivez le titre!
d Ouvrez la fenêtre!
e Fermez la porte!
f Frappez à la porte!

4 **a** Écoute!
b Regarde!
c Lis le titre!
d Ouvre la fenêtre!
e Ferme la porte!
f Frappe à la porte!

6 Tu comprends?
a Asseyez-vous!
b Viens ici!
c Assieds-toi!
d Taisez-vous!
e Regardez!
f Regarde!
g Écoutez!
h Lève-toi!
i Range tes affaires!
j Rangez vos affaires!

Point 19 *Au, à la, à l'* and *aux*

1 **a** les toilettes
b la piscine
c la gare
d l'hôtel
e le cinéma
f le café

3 Tu comprends?
Jon adore aller aux magasins. Pour acheter un journal, il va au tabac. Pour le pain, il va à la boulangerie. Il va à la boucherie pour la viande, et à la pâtisserie pour des gâteaux. Pour les boîtes de conserve, il va au supermarché et pour les fruits, il s'arrête au marché. Parfois, il va à l'épicerie. Avant de rentrer à la maison il prend un verre au café.

Point 20 *Du, de la, de l' and des*

1 *He has ...*
some cheese
some sugar
some flour
some meat
some mineral water
some Orangina
some bananas
some eggs

3 Tu comprends?

a «Je voudrais du poulet, s'il vous plaît.»
b «Je voudrais aussi du fromage, s'il vous plaît.»
c «Et avec ça, de l'eau minérale, s'il vous plaît.»
d «Avez-vous des œufs, s'il vous plaît?»
e «Je voudrais aussi de la farine, s'il vous plaît.»
f «Je voudrais des bananes, s'il vous plaît.»
g «Et avec ça du sel, s'il vous plaît.»
h «Je voudrais aussi de l'Orangina, s'il vous plaît.»
i «Donnez-moi de la bière, s'il vous plaît.»
j «Et je dois prendre du thé.»

Point 21 *À côté de la banque mais en face du café*

3 Tu comprends?

a Le restaurant est en face de la banque.
b Le restaurant est à côté de la laverie.
c La banque est à côté du tabac.
d Le tabac est en face de l'épicerie.
e La boucherie est en face des toilettes.
f La boucherie est à côté des taxis.
g Les taxis sont en face de la boulangerie.
h Les toilettes sont à côté de la boulangerie.
i La laverie est en face du café.
j La boulangerie est en face des taxis.

Point 22 *Ne... plus, ne... rien and ne... jamais*

3 Tu comprends?

a Je ne vois rien.
b Je n'ai plus de carottes.
c Je ne parle jamais en classe.

d Je ne joue plus au football.
e Je ne joue jamais au football.
f Je ne joue rien.
g Je ne regrette rien.
h Je ne dis rien.
i Je ne vais jamais au cinéma.
j Je ne vais plus au cinéma.

Point 23 The Past Perfect Tense with regular verbs

4 **a** Elle a chanté.
b Nous avons regardé un bon film.
c J'ai discuté avec mes copains.
d Tu as dansé?
e Vous avez joué au foot?
f Il a travaillé en classe.
g Nous avons gagné le match.
h Tu as refusé.
i Il a triché.
j Ils ont pêché les truites.

6 Tu comprends?

Le travail au collège a fini à trois heures et demie. Martine a fini ses devoirs à la maison. André a rencontré Martine devant le cinéma à sept heures et demie. Ils ont regardé le film ensemble. Le film était triste et les deux jeunes gens ont pleuré pendant deux heures. Après le film, ils ont décidé d'aller au 'Café des Jeunes Amoureux' ensemble. Martine a choisi un coca et Jean-Claude a préféré un Orangina. Cinq minutes plus tard, André a commandé une bière blonde mais la serveuse a répondu:

– André, tu es trop jeune, finis ton Orangina et emmène ta copine chez elle!

Ils sont partis ensemble. Devant sa maison, Martine a embrassé André. André était fou de joie. Les deux jeunes gens étaient amoureux!

24 The Past Perfect Tense with irregular verbs

3 Tu comprends?

a J'ai pris mon petit déjeuner.
b Elle a dit au revoir.
c J'ai reçu une lettre.

d Il a vu la tour Eiffel.
e Nous avons fait nos devoirs.
f Vous avez lu le journal?
g Tu as compris?
h J'ai bien dormi, merci.
i Ils ont dû partir.
j On a fait la vaisselle ensemble.

25 The Past Perfect Tense with *être*

4 **a** Nous sommes descendus du bus.
b Ils sont partis.
c Elles sont allées au cinéma.
d Vous êtes partis en vitesse.
e Nous sommes restés à la maison.
f Ils sont montés dans le bus.
g Elles sont arrivées à neuf heures.
h Ils sont morts.
i Vous êtes nés.
j Nous sommes tombés amoureux.

5 **Tu comprends?**
Ils ont pris leur petit déjeuner à sept heures et demie. Ils ont quitté la maison à huit heures pour aller à la gare. Ils sont montés dans le train à huit heures et quart. Peu après, ils sont arrivés à leur destination. Ils sont descendus du train. Ils sont arrivés au collège dix minutes plus tard. Ils ont discuté avec leurs copains dans la cour. Ils sont entrés dans la classe. À neuf heures, les cours ont commencé. Le collège a fini à trois heures et demie.

Point 26 The Past Perfect Tense with reflexive verbs

3 **a** Je me suis réveillé/e.
b Elle s'est levée.
c Ils se sont habillés.
d Il s'est rasé.
e Elles se sont promenées.
f Je me suis couché.
g Tu t'es douché/e?
h Elle s'est lavée.

4 Tu comprends?

Nous nous sommes réveillés assez tôt, vers sept heures. Nous nous sommes habillés et nous nous sommes lavés. Vers sept heures et demie nous avons pris le petit déjeuner - c'est d'habitude du toast avec du thé. Nous avons quitté la maison vers huit heures pour aller au collége. Nous sommes arrivés au collège vers huit heures et demie. À cinq heures du soir nous sommes rentrés à la maison. Nous avons pris le dîner vers sept heures. Nous avons fait nos devoirs et nous nous sommes couchés.

Point 27 Making comparisons and superlatives

2 **a** La France est plus grande que l'Angleterre.
b L'Angleterre est plus grande que l'Irlande.
c Je suis moins riche que la reine.
d La tour de Blackpool est moins haute que la tour Eiffel.
e Une Rolls Royce est plus chère qu'une Mini.
f Une souris est moins grosse qu'un éléphant.
g Pierre est aussi intelligent que Françoise.
h Marie est aussi forte que Michel.
i Michel est aussi stupide que Marie.
j Le français est moins difficile que le chinois.

3 Tu comprends?

a L'Angleterre est moins grande que la France.
b L'Irlande est moins grande que L'Angleterre.
c La reine est plus riche que moi.
d La tour Eiffel est plus haute que la tour de Blackpool.
e Une Mini est moins chère qu'une Rolls Royce.
f Un éléphant est plus gros qu'une souris.
g Françoise est aussi intelligente que Pierre.
h Michel est aussi fort que Marie.
i Marie est aussi stupide que Michel.
j Le chinois est plus difficile que le français.

6 Tu comprends?

a Entre la France et l'Angleterre, la France est la plus grande.
b Entre l'Angleterre et l'Irlande, l'Angleterre est la plus grande.
c Entre moi et la reine, je suis le/la moins riche.
d Entre la tour Eiffel et la Tour de Blackpool, la tour Eiffel est la plus haute.

e Entre une Mini et une Rolls Royce, une Mini est la moins chère.
f Entre un éléphant et une souris, une souris est la moins grosse.
g Entre Françoise et Suzanne, Suzanne est la moins grande/la plus petite.
h Entre Michel et Jean, Jean est le moins grand/le plus petit.
i Entre Marie et Françoise, Françoise est la plus grande.
j Entre le français et le chinois, le chinois est le plus difficile.

Point 28 Object pronouns

3 **a** Je la déteste.
b Je les déteste.
c Elle les adore.
d Nous l'adorons.
e Tu le lis?
f Je les mange.
g Je vais la voir.
h Nous allons la voir.
i Je l'ai vu.
j Je l'ai aimé.

5 Tu comprends?
a Oui, je les aime.
b Oui, je la vois.
c Oui, je les fais.
d Oui, je le prends.
e Oui, je vais le voir.
f Oui, je vais la chanter.
g Oui, je l'ai vu.
h Oui, nous l'avons vu trois fois.
i Oui, je l'ai pris.
j Oui, je l'ai fini.

7 Tu comprends?

a	*I am writing to her.*	Je lui écris.
b	*I am writing to them.*	Je leur écris.
c	*I am giving them a present.*	Je leur offre un cadeau.
d	*I'm going to see her.*	Je vais la voir.
e	*I'm going to speak to them.*	Je vais leur parler.
f	*I spoke to them in French.*	Je leur ai parlé en français.
g	*I wrote to them in French.*	Je leur ai écrit en français.
h	*I answered them.*	Je leur ai répondu.
i	*I asked them for an ice cream.*	Je leur ai demandé une glace.
j	*I asked him for an ice cream.*	Je lui ai demandé une glace.

9 Tu comprends?

- **a** Je t'écris.
- **b** Tu me parles?
- **c** Elle m'aime.
- **d** Elle nous déteste.
- **e** Je vais t'écrire/vous écrire.
- **f** Elle m'a écrit.
- **g** Il nous a vus/vues.
- **h** Monsieur, je vous ai vu.
- **i** Elle m'a répondu.
- **j** Jean-Michel, je t'ai vu.

Point 29 *Ne... personne* and *ne... que*

4
- **a** je n'ai pris que deux croissants
- **b** il n'a rien vu
- **c** je n'ai vu personne
- **d** je ne regrette rien
- **e** il ne va voir personne
- **f** je n'ai vu que trois personnes
- **g** je n'aime que toi
- **h** nous n'aimons personne
- **i** le facteur n'a livré qu'une lettre
- **j** nous n'avons jamais compris

5 Tu comprends?

- **a** Je ne regarde jamais la télé.
- **b** Je n'aime personne.
- **c** Je n'aime que toi.
- **d** Je n'ai pas joué.
- **e** Je n'ai jamais joué.
- **f** Je n'ai joué qu'une fois.
- **g** Elle n'a rien vu.
- **h** Elle n'a vu personne.
- **i** Nous n'avons vu que les actualités.
- **j** Il n'a tué personne.

Point 30 Venir de

2 Il vient de manquer son bus. (a)
Il vient de prendre un bain. (b)
Il vient de téléphoner. (c)
Il vient de se lever. (d)
Il vient de déjeuner. (e)
Il vient de voir un fantôme. (f)

3 **a** Je viens de prendre un bain.
b Nous venons de prendre une douche.
c Ils viennent de voir un fantôme.
d Vous venez de vous lever.
e Tu viens de manquer le bus.
f Je viens de prendre une douche.

4 Tu comprends?
a Je viens de manger.
b Je viens de boire une limonade.
c Je viens de faire 10km à pied.
d Je viens d'acheter un dictionnaire.
e Je viens de gagner 1000F.
f Je viens de mettre le radiateur.
g Je viens de mourir.
h Je viens de voir un fantôme.
i Je viens de téléphoner chez le dentiste.
j Je viens de faire mes devoirs.

Point 31 Using *y*

2 Je vais en Espagne avec mes amis.
J'y vais avec mes amis.
Je vais au cinéma ce soir.
J'y vais ce soir.
Tu vas au match de foot avec ta correspondante?
Tu y vas avec ta correspondante?
Vous écrivez souvent en France?
Vous y écrivez souvent?
Ils retournent à la maison.
Ils y retournent?
Il rentre en Angleterre.
Il y rentre.
Elle reste chez elle.
Elle y reste.
Elle va souvent à la disco.
Elle y va souvent.
Elles dansent beaucoup à la disco.
Elles y dansent beaucoup.
Vous allez au restaurant avec nous?
Vous y allez avec nous?

4 Tu comprends?

- L'année dernière j'ai pris des vacances à Paris. Je y suis allé avec mes parents. Il y a fait très mauvais donc nous avons passé notre temps dans les grands magasins. En plus, nous y avons vu toutes les curiosités.
- Cette année je reste en Angleterre. Il y fait beau donc je vais à la plage tous les weekends. J'y joue dans l'eau avec mes amis. Tu y vas souvent ?
- L'année prochaine, je vais retourner à Paris mais cette fois je vais y aller avec mes copains. On va y voir tous les magasins de disques. Tu vas y aller avec moi?

Point 32 Using *en*

1 **a** Oui, il y en a un. (*Yes, there is one.*)
b Oui, il y en a un.
c Il y en a deux.
d Il y en a trois.
e Il y en a trois.
f Il y en a une.
g Oui, il y en a un.
h Oui, il y en a une.

2 Tu comprends?
a Oui, j'en ai trois.
b Oui, j'en ai.
c Non, je n'en ai pas.
d Oui, il y en a.
e Oui, j'en ai deux.
f Non, je n'en ai pas.
g Non, je n'en ai pas.
h Oui, j'en ai beaucoup.

Point 33 *Qui* and *que*

2 **a** C'est le vin que j'aime le plus.
b C'est ce vin qui est le meilleur de la région.
c Ce sont les vacances que j'adore.
d Ce sont les vacances qui coûtent cher.
e Il y a la montagne qui vous offre un peu de tout.
f C'est surtout la montagne que je préfère.
g En plus, il y a plage qui n'est pas loin.
h C'est cette plage-ci que préfèrent mes enfants.

3 Tu comprends?

J'y suis arrivé. Je suis entré dans le café que je connais depuis longtemps. Le garçon que je vois chaque été était là. Il m'a vu et il a dit:

– C'est bien le cycliste qui vient nous voir tous les ans?

Tout d'un coup, j'entends une autre voix que je reconnais. C'était la femme que j'avais rencontrée pendant mes vacances. La serveuse qui nous connaissait était au coin de la salle peu allumée. Elle a mis un disque. On entendait une voix qui chantait 'Te souviens-tu d'un slow?'. Et puis, j'entends:

– Jean-Claude, c'est bien toi que je vois?
– Oui, c'est moi, Claudine!

La femme qui m'avait écrit tous les jours depuis un an était dans mes bras. C'est bien elle qui m'a épousé!

Point 34 The Imperfect Tense and distinguishing it from the Past Perfect

2 **a** enjoy - Imperfect; **b** came - Perfect; **c** spoilt - Perfect; **d** sing - Imperfect; **e** play - Imperfect; **f** work - Imperfect; **g** would have a good time - Imperfect; **h** had some fun - Perfect; **i** wasn't - Imperfect; **j** done - Perfect.

4 **a** Je chantais.
b Elle dansait.
c Nous travaillions/on travaillait.
d Il faisait du soleil.
e Ils pleuraient.
f Je buvais.
g Elle écrivait.
h Il avait mal à la tête.
i Elle partait.
j Il déjeunait.

7 Tu comprends?

Quand j'étais petit, j'allais au bord de la mer tous les weekends. Une fois j'ai décidé d'aller à la campagne. Comme il faisait beau, j'ai pris mon maillot de bain. Quand nous sommes arrivés il pleuvait. Nous n'étions pas contents. Nous avons mangé dans un restaurant pas trop cher. C'était bien. Nous avons quitté le restaurant assez tard et nous sommes arrivés chez nous très fatigués.

Point 35 *Pour* + infinitive

2 **a** Je suis allé au café pour boire un coup.
b Ils sont allés à la piscine pour nager.
c Elle est allée à la disco pour danser.
d Nous sommes allés au jardin public pour nous promener un peu.
e On est allé au cinéma pour regarder un bon film.
f Nous sommes allés au restaurant pour bien manger.
g Je suis allé au syndicat d'initiative pour demander un plan de la ville.
h Elle est allée à la boucherie pour acheter de la viande.
i Il est allé au stade pour regarder le match.
j Je suis allé au lit pour dormir.

3 Tu comprends?
a J'ai téléphoné à l'hôtel pour réserver une chambre.
b J'ai pris le train pour aller à Londres.
c Je suis allé au jardin public pour rencontrer ma petite amie.
d Je suis allée à la pâtisserie pour acheter un gâteau délicieux.
e Nous sommes allés à la poste pour prendre des timbres.
f Nous avons passé par le parking pour laisser la voiture.
g On nous a offert du champagne pour fêter le premier de l'an.
h Nous avons passé par le port pour voir le bateau.
i Ma mère s'est arrêtée à la charcuterie pour prendre du saucisson.
j Je me suis arrêté pour aller aux toilettes.

Point 36 *Après avoir* + past participle

4 **a** Après m'être levé, je me suis lavé.
b Après m'être habillé, j'ai rangé mes affaires.
c Après avoir pris mon petit déjeuner, j'ai quitté la maison.
d Après avoir marché un peu, je suis arrivé au collège.
e Après être arrivé dans la cour, j'ai rencontré mes copains.
f Après avoir discuté pendant quelques minutes, je suis entré avec les autres.
g J'ai pris mon déjeuner à la maison après avoir travaillé pendant toute la matinée.
h Après avoir fini à quatre heures, j'ai décidé de prendre un verre.

5 Tu comprends?

a Après avoir chargé la voiture, je me suis mis en route.
b Après être arrivé au port, je me suis présenté aux Passeports.
c Après avoir trouvé ma cabine, j'ai dormi un peu.

d Après m'être habillé, je suis allé à la disco.
e Après avoir dansé un peu, je me suis couché.
f Après être descendu du bateau, j'ai pris la route pour le camping.
g Après avoir dressé la tente, j'ai préparé un repas.
h Après avoir fait du soleil, il a beaucoup plu.
i Après avoir sauvé ma tente, j'ai chargé ma voiture.
j Après être rentré, j'ai pris un bain.

Point 37 *Avant de* + infinitive

2 **a** Je me réveille à sept heures, avant de me lever.
b Avant de quitter la maison, je prends mon petit déjeuner.
c J'attends à l'arrêt, avant de prendre le bus.
d Je discute avec mes copains dans la cour, avant d'entrer.
e Je rentre chez moi avant de déjeuner.
f Avant de retourner au collège, je prends mon dessert.
g Le soir, je rentre vers quatre heures et demie, avant de dîner.
h Avant de jouer avec mes copains je fais mes devoirs.
i Je mets mon pyjama avant d'aller au lit.
j Avant de m'endormir, je lis jusqu'à ce que je sois fatigué.

3 **Tu comprends?**

b Il faut chauffer la théière avant d'ajouter du thé.
c Il faut ajouter de l'eau bouillante avant d'attendre trois minutes.
d Il faut mettre un peu de lait dans les tasses avant de verser le thé.
e Il faut ajouter du sucre si on en prend avant de tourner le thé dans la tasse.
f Il faut lever le petit doigt avant de goûter son thé.

Point 38 The Future Tense

4 **a** Il finira son travail à cinq heures.
b Je finirai .....
c Je regarderai .....
d J'arriverai .....
e Je descendrai ....
f Il m'attendra .....
g Nous choisirons .....
h Nous discuterons .....
i Nous rentrerons .....
j Nous nous coucherons .....

6 Tu comprends?

Je prendrai mes vacances en France avec mes copains. Mes parents iront en Espagne. Ils passeront leurs vacances dans un hôtel - avec salle de bains, un bar, une disco, une piscine chauffée, etc. Moi, je ferai du camping. Nous y irons en autostop. Ma mère n'aimera pas tellement ça mais ce ne sera pas cher! Mes parents partiront en avion, bien sûr! Nous nous amuserons tous en vacances et, en plus, ma sœur aînée aura la tranquillité de la maison en Angleterre!

Point 39 The Conditional Tense

5 **a** J'irais chez le dentiste.
b Je prendrais de l'aspirine.
c J'achèterais une moto.
d Je ferais des devoirs.
e J'irais en Espagne.
f Je me coucherais.
g Je mangerais.
h Je boirais.
i Je prendrais un bain.
j Je mettrais un manteau.

6 Tu comprends?

a Elle a promis qu'elle le ferait demain.
b Il a dit qu'il téléphonerait la semaine prochaine.
c Ils m'ont dit qu'ils iraient au match.
d Elle m'a dit qu'elle m'achèterait un nouveau blouson.
e Tu m'as dit que tu n'y travaillerais plus.
f Elle m'a répondu qu'elle ne se lèverait jamais.
g J'ai dit au prof que je refuserais de le faire.
h Le Premier Ministre nous a dit qu'il nous dirait toujours la vérité.
i Elle a dit qu'elle verrait le docteur demain.
j Elles ont dit qu'elles se réveilleraient de bonne heure.

Point 40 An Introduction to the Subjunctive

5 Tu comprends?

a Bien que je sois jeune, je suis intelligent.
b Bien que je sois jeune, je suis sensible.
c Bien que j'aie mal à la tête, j'y vais quand même.
d Bien que je fasse mes devoirs, je n'apprends rien.

e Bien que je sache le faire, je ne veux pas jouer!
f Bien que je t'écrive, je ne t'aime plus.

6 **a** À condition que je travaille, je réussirai.
b À condition que je fasse mes devoirs, je réussirai.
c À condition que je me couche tard, je serai fatigué.
d À condition qu'il y aille, il sera content.
e À condition que nous finissions à l'heure, nous viendrons.
f À condition qu'il soit sage, il pourra venir.

8 Tu comprends?
a Il faut que tu promènes le chien!
b Il faut que tu ranges ta chambre.
c Il faut que tu fasses tes devoirs.
d Il faut que tu prennes ton dîner.
e Il faut que tu débarrasses la table.
f Il faut que tu te laves.

9 Tu comprends?
a Il est possible que je sois chômeur.
b Il est possible que je me marie.
c Il est possible que nous ayons des enfants.
d Il est possible que nous allions à l'étranger.
e Il est possible que nous soyons patrons.
f Il est possible que tu rêves?

11 Tu comprends?
a Je veux que tu m'écrives pour confirmer que tu viens.
b Je veux que tu portes ton blouson rouge pour t'identifier.
c Je veux que tu apportes du vin pour papa.
d Je veux que tu sois à l'heure.
e Je veux que tu ailles au Bureau de Change devant quai numéro 6.
f Je veux que tu me parles doucement en français.
g Je veux que tu prennes tous tes repas avec nous.
h Je veux que tu arrêtes de fumer en Angleterre.

Point 41 An Introduction to the Past Historic

3 *First structure:*
a Elle écouta un disque.
b Il regarda un bon film.
c Nous rentrâmes tard.

Second structure:
d Ils choisirent un livre.
e Nous finîmes notre travail.

And others:
f Je bus un coca.
g Ils firent leur travail.
h Je vis la tour Eiffel.
i Il vint à pied.
j Elle sortit.

4 Tu comprends?

Pierre se leva de bonne heure. Il quitta la maison après avoir pris son petit déjeuner. Il devait rencontrer Monique pour la première fois devant le Café de la Ville. Il dut passer aux magasins d'abord. Il alla à la boucherie pour acheter le poulet. Ensuite, il passa par la boulangerie. Il se précipita vers la gare. Il prit le bus. Malheureusement, il y avait de la circulation. Il regarda sa montre. Tout d'un coup, le bus s'arrêta. Voilà, elle était là. Ils s'embrassèrent. Ils s'écrivaient depuis six ans.